The Wizard's Guide to Energy Healing

The Wizard's Guide to Energy Healing

Introducing the Divine Healing Secrets of Merlin

Brett Bevell

Monkfish Book Publishing Company
Rhinebeck, NY

Library of Congress Control Number: 2015912851

Paperback ISBN: 978-1-939681-49-2
eBook ISBN: 978-1-939681-50-8

Printed in the United States of America

Book design by Colin Rolfe
Cover design by Chris Hallman

Monkfish Book Publishing Company
22 East Market Street, Suite 304
Rhinebeck, NY 12572
www.monkfishpublishing.com

For my beloved wife Helema and our son Dylan,

and the amazing light that shines through each of you!

Acknowledgments

I would like to acknowledge those teachers and mentors on my journey who encouraged me to trust my creativity, intuition and inner guidance, including John Perkins, David Morehouse, Llyn Roberts, Alex Grey, Allyson Grey, Iyanla Van Zant, Alberto Vilolldo, and Nina Spiro. Also, I offer a special acknowledgment to Alexandra Marquardt and Ric Weinman, the first teachers who opened me to the Divine energy healing magic of Merlin. I also thank my teacher and dear friend, the late shaman Carolion, who took my consciousness to the furthest reaches in her dreamwork classes, devic gardening classes, and who showed me a higher purpose through her dedication to using energy healing and shamanic practice to promote world peace. As well I wish to give thanks to my fellow teachers in Magical Awakening® (Magical Awakening is a service mark of Brett Bevell) who have been dear loyal friends on this journey: James Philips, Hethyrre, Michele Denis, Michael Marlowe, Lori Avalon and Justin Prim. Let me thank as well the whimsical poet and Magical Awakening wizard Meghann Plunkett, who kindly agreed to read this book before I wrote it so I could finally give focus and intention to this writing project that I delayed for many years. Finally, I want to give thanks to my dear beloved, my wife Helema Kadir, who makes each day being on this Earth truly joyful to me: as tempting as it may be for me to live in other realms she keeps me grounded in this one much of the time.

Table of Contents

Introduction

Step with me into the following chapters of this book and I will take you on an amazing journey that will explore the furthest reaches of consciousness and energy healing. I do not ask you to take this leap blindly, but to simply try the exercises outlined in the following chapters and let your own experience be the litmus test. I have found as a teacher of various modes of energy healing, including Reiki, that the Magical Awakening® Energy Healing System is by far my preferred energy healing method. It is not only highly effective in helping one quickly move through spiritual, physical, and emotional life issues, but it also is designed to awaken the practitioner wizard to their own Divine essence, an essence which exists in everyone but which many are often asleep to.

You are loved by the Divine. You are so loved by the Divine that the Divine wants nothing more of you than for you to know how loved and magical you truly are. The Magical Awakening® Energy Healing System does not assume you are broken and need to be fixed, an unfortunate focus of some energy healing modalities. Instead, it assumes you are a wonderful child of the Divine, and all that the Divine wants you to know is your own connection to that Divine love and Divine magic that created this universe.

Magical Awakening work can be used to clear away negative energy, undo self-destructive thought patterns, spiritually heal emotional trauma, and bring restorative healing into our physical bodies. Yet much more than this, it teaches you a magical way of being that involves playing energetically with the Divine. As you play more and more with the Divine in this energetic way, you become spiritually free on all levels. You lose those fears that have taught you to be less than the magical being that you are.

The system itself is based on play, on deep intuitive listening, and on knowing that no harm can come from using this form of Divine energy healing. There is no test nor are there any symbols to memorize. There is no spiritual allegiance you need to make to me or to anyone else. The system itself is designed to empower you to find your own way, to claim your own power, and to know the magical inheritance that is naturally yours as a conscious being beloved by the Divine.

Our modern culture has been built around a deep worship of science, intellect, and reason, and so it is entirely natural if you question the levels of healing and spiritual awakening offered through this work. Yet science already tells us that we are all made of energy. Einstein knew this when he wrote his famous formula $E=MC^2$, which in layman's terms simply says that everything is made of energy, even matter, which is simply energy in its most dense form. Yet I know the power of social conditioning. And it can be challenging to override the overt social messages we receive from our family, friends, parents, and teachers telling us that magic does not exists— making many of us what the author JK Rowling refers to in her Harry Potter series as *muggles*. We have seen what this muggle form of consciousness has done to our world, how it has robbed us of honoring the Divine magic that is intricately woven into all aspects of creation.

If you engage this work, and treat it as a journey of creative play with the Divine, it will positively change the way you see our world. It will help you release old wounds, past and present traumas, as well as mental and social conditioning that may be limiting your sense of what is possible. Let go of your preconceptions, whatever they may be, and simply trust your own experience as you engage this profound work. Simply allow your heart to open as child, and play. Begin that spirit of play now by simply touching the question mark below for at least thirty seconds and see if the magic held inside of it changes your consciousness.

Chapter 1
What Is Energy Healing?

THE UNIVERSE IS CONSCIOUS. I first recognized this two decades ago when I began engaging a number of alternative healing techniques to overcome my own childhood trauma, trauma which was complex and deep, far too complex for traditional psychotherapy to conveniently unwind. As I engaged these techniques, which ranged from shamanic healing to rebirthing to energy healing, I noticed quick and radical changes that were very positive begin to happen in my own life. I also noticed my own level of awareness grew, my intuition became more sharp, and I was overcome with the constant peculiar sense that the universe was conscious and aware of me. The deeper down I went exploring these alternative methods of healing, the better I felt about myself and my body, and my emotional awareness grew. I was able to eventually feel the energetic attachments between me and those who had abused me decades ago. I was then taught how to sever and release those attachments, these energetic strings that had kept me like a puppet victim for so many years no matter how much traditional therapy I did. Once those attachments were cut, I felt empowered to be free and have been on an amazing journey ever since.

Energy healing works with the premise that everything in existence is made of light and has an energetic signature. This concept corresponds with the string theory in modern physics that the smallest, most basic particles of creation are oscillating and vibrating, almost like the music from the strings of a guitar. These energy signatures affect us all the time. If we are in a room that is full of joy, we feel that *vibration*. Similarly, if you enter a room where people have been fighting and arguing it often holds a very different energetic signature, what some might call *bad vibes*. What energy healing does is address those fundamental energetic signatures, even those energetic signatures from the past that can impact the present and future.

My own healing journey taught me that though I cannot change the past I have been able to radically shift and alter how those energetic signatures from the past impact me now. We cannot change past events, but we can change the notes, the tune that those strings from the past are sending into the future. We can also change the energetic signatures of our own cells for physical healing, as well as change the energetic signatures in our emotions to change how we feel about ourselves and the world.

Some schools of energy healing such as the very popular form called Reiki use a primary energetic signature to alter or shift a person into a place of well being. You might think of Reiki as a constant single energetic note that clears out and harmonizes the other energetic signatures at play in a person's energy field. Reiki at higher levels can also bring in a few different energetic signatures by using sacred Reiki symbols that deepen a healing even more. Other forms of energy healing also have their own energetic signature, such as the Light of the Eternal One work in my previous book *Energy Healing for Everyone*, which has an energetic signature designed to help a person remember their own connection to the Divine. The Magical Awakening® Energy Healing System has an almost infinite expression of energetic signatures available, which gives the healer an opportunity to creatively work with the Divine consciousness in ways that are challenging to put into words given how vast and expansive these healing opportunities are.

Such a level of healing changes radically the approach of a healer, given the numerous energetic signatures one has access to. Unlike Reiki or other modalities where there is a structured set of hand positions and routines for any given healing session, Magical Awakening calls upon the healer to allow their consciousness be guided by the energy itself, so that each session is entirely unique and geared to the person receiving it. A Magical Awakening healing session is actually quite creative from the healer's point of view. The healer goes into a place of deep listening, allowing the Divine consciousness within the energy itself to unfold and teach the healer what needs to happen next. It is more a healing art and not a science. This also allows the healer to let go of their ego, let go of the need to fix or heal anyone. Instead, they are simply playing with numerous Divine energetic signatures the same way a musician riffs on various notes during a jazz improv session. The beauty and joy of this is often felt as much by the healer as the person being healed, though the positive healing results for the person receiving the healing are astonishing. One person whom I gave three treatments to told me it changed their life and that they no longer felt the need to be in therapy after fifteen years. Also, a Magical Awakening session can be sent to numerous people simultaneously. At Omega Institute, where I work and teach, I often give half hour long sessions to a room of twenty or more people all simultaneously, and have on rare occasion worked on as many as one hundred people at once.

Energy healing at this level leads the healer into awakened states of consciousness, often being able to see karmic patterns, past life issues, and even the core spark of Divinity residing inside each person. As you learn to unwind the debris that covers that core spark, more light begins to shine outward into all aspects of your life. You also begin to realize that the universe itself is a dream, a playful dream. As a healer, you loosen, let go, laugh, and come to realize you are playing with the Divine and nothing more, that the joy of energy healing at its deepest level is simply energetic play, a game with the Divine. I do not even think of Magical Awakening healers as being practitioners as much as wizards, like the great wizard Merlin.

Magical Awakening has its roots in the lineage of Merlin and the healing power of The Grail. The beauty of this system is that not only is it one of the most powerful energy healing systems I have been shown in terms of what one can accomplish with it, but it also works to free the mind of the wizard healer who uses it. Magical Awakening always requires that the wizard healer be fully present, open as a child, without preconceptions to where the healing is going to go. The wizard healer is asked to listen intuitively to the energy itself, and to play with it. Through this sense of magical play it is constantly reinforcing that the universe itself is a dream, a playful dream. We are nothing but haikus, little wonderful poems created by Divine imagination. It is through this playful dance that we realize we are nothing at all, and we then know simultaneously that we are everything.

Just to continue in a wizard's spirit of play, if you would like to experience yourself inside a bubble of Divine consciousness, simply put your finger inside the zero and keep it there as long as you wish:

Chapter 2
The God-wizard Merlin and The Goddess Known as Lady of the Lake

Merlin is more than just a myth, more than just single wizard living at a point in human history. Merlin is a male expression of Divine magical consciousness. That is why the tales of Camelot and Arthurian legend are so alive still. One of the energy healing lineages I have studied claims that there have been many Merlins throughout human history, and that their wisdom and power can be traced back to an avatar, a human incarnation of the Divine who lived thousands of years ago in India named Mahindra, and who embodied that Divine magic and brought it to the planet, similar to the way Jesus embodied Divine love and brought it to Earth. That particular energy healing system is quite advanced and very powerful, and there is no reason for me to think that their claim is untrue. Yet I also believe that the power of Merlin (or Mahindra) is not limited to just one healing system, and that the expression of Divine energy healing is far too vast to be limited or contained within one modality. Magical Awakening has been revealed to me as a healing system that embraces not only the Divine masculine aspect of magical consciousness known as Merlin but the Divine feminine aspect of magical consciousness as well. In my work with Magical Awakening I have been introduced to that powerful expression of Divine magical consciousness that is female and also omnipresent. That expression is revealed as Lady of the Lake.

Lady of the Lake and Merlin oversee Magical Awakening and are the guardians of this Divine healing system. In Arthurian legends there are many stories of Lady of the Lake, as well as different names for her such as Nimue or Viviane. Some even mention Lady of the Lake walking on water, a magical ability (miracle) usually only accomplished by an avatar, an incarnation of the Divine, like Jesus. But let's suppose that there had been a living female avatar, a female incarnation of the Divine, at the time of King Arthur, who could do things such as walk on water. How might legends of such a powerful female be passed down in a time where women in general were disempowered and held a far lesser status than men? Would the patriarchy of that time even consider the idea of a female incarnation of the Divine? The author Caitlin Matthews proposes in her book *Ladies of the Lake* that the patriarchy of Arthurian legends simply fragments the Celtic Goddess archetypes through a patriarchal lens that maligns some of them. I am neither a historian nor student of medieval literature, but instead a wizard healer. I learn what I know through direct experience and by magically exploring the multi-dimensional realities of an issue. And, in working with the Magical Awakening energies, my intuition tells me that Lady of the Lake lived on Earth as a powerful female avatar-like being at the time of King Arthur, and could do things such as walk on water. Her presence was positive, and just as some of the stories about Jesus became edited or distorted over time so too it is likely that the legends about Lady of the Lake underwent similar patriarchal editing, edited to the point where she was no longer seen as a benevolent healing Goddess or even a real living person, just a myth. When I ask Lady of the Lake directly who she is, this is her answer:

I am the birth and the sound of woman. I am that which hears you when you are sleeping, and that which speaks through the call of birds at dawn. I am the earth herself, the beauty of the land, the mystery of the night sky. I am the ready made love that is always willing to bring healing and solace. I am the spark of light that exists inside a mother's womb. I am Isis, Mary, Lakshmi, the infinite Goddess of all creation. Here I am in this form, speaking now. But know I am limitless, beyond measure.

As the female expression of Divine magical consciousness, at least within the Magical Awakening system, Lady of the Lake is a guide, and perhaps the true source of this system's healing power. She is more mysterious than Merlin, and thus requires a bit more of an introduction. Merlin, as the male expression of Divine magical

8

consciousness, works with Lady of the Lake. They are co-creators, guides, and similarly one in the same. Just as we are simultaneously emptiness and everything, so too are they the male and female faces of the ultimate Divine mystery. They are simultaneously the same being, and yet not the same being. These Divine intelligences will always be there for you once you become empowered to the first level of this system, whispering their guidance continuously. The real trick is daring to listen! Because often the guidance they offer transcends reason. But by being in the moment, and listening deep within, you will be guided. It is your choice whether or not to listen to that guidance.

If you would like an energetic taste of Divine mystery. Simply place your finger between the parenthesis below:

Chapter 3
The Three Cauldrons

This wizardly system of healing called Magical Awakening is designed to bring you closer to knowing that Divine spark that is you. Much of that happens through a sense of magical energetic play with the Divine. The first level of this system offers you access to three primary energy centers, known as the three cauldrons. In Celtic shamanism there were three primary energy centers said to exist within the human body: one at the belly, one at the heart and one at the top of the head. The one at the belly was an energy center called Coire Goiriath, the cauldron of warming. The energy of this cauldron maintained the health of the physical body. The second cauldron, near the heart, in the center of a person's chest, ruled a person's vocation in life and was called Coire Emma. The third cauldron, the cauldron of knowledge, existed at the top of a person's head and was called Coire Sois. Although these cauldrons exist in everyone's energy system, similar to chakras, and can be accessed by anyone who is sufficiently trained in the appropriate Celtic shamanic technique, these are not exactly the same cauldrons that are used in the Magical Awakening system. I mention them simply for historical reference and because they are related to, but not the same as, the three cauldrons in Magical Awakening.

The three cauldrons in Magical Awakening are not something that already exist in everyone. These three cauldrons are Divine energetic devices created in a wizard during the first empowerment in the Magical Awakening system. They are different from the three cauldrons of Celtic shamanism in several ways. First, the cauldrons in Magical Awakening are a direct link to Divine magical energy, whereas the three cauldrons mentioned in Celtic shamanism are more like chakras, energy wheels that reflect our own personal energetic health and evolution. The cauldron at the belly in Magical Awakening flows a very fiery hot energy we wizards call Dragon Fire. This energy can be used to help maintain the physical body by rooting out disease on the spiritual level, but it also has other uses, such as purifying the energy in a room, clearing away negative entities and thoughts, and basically burning away anything energetically that is not for a person's highest good. The second cauldron in Magical Awakening, like Coire Emma, exists near the region of the heart, near the center of a person's chest, and is called the Grail. But, it has little to do with a person's vocation and instead flows a wonderful restorative healing energy directly from the Divine. This cauldron is also used for integration, using a technique that will be revealed later in this book. The third cauldron in Magical Awakening is called Arthur's Crown. Like its Celtic shamanic counterpart Coire Sois, it is about knowledge and our connection to the Divine, but takes it a step further. In Magical Awakening a wizard can actually flow energy from Arthur's Crown to "wake up" energy that is misguided, or thought-forms that perhaps have lost their true origin. It essentially reminds things energetically of their own true Divine nature.

These three cauldrons in Magical Awakening access Divine energy, and, like Reiki or other forms of Divine energy healing, are not relying on a person's individual energy. Once you receive the first wizard empowerment you will be able to access these energies for life, at will, as long as your intention is for the highest good. If your intention is not for the highest good, these cauldrons will simply not allow their energy to come forth.

Once you receive the empowerment in the following chapter you will be able to use these cauldrons of Magical Awakening for self healing and also to send energy to others, to assist individuals or groups, and to send healing to the earth, the land, and the oceans, restoring your own healing connection to the web of all life.

If you would like to experience a thirty minute Magical Awakening session before engaging the wizard empowerment in the following chapter, just touch the fingertip on the following page for a few seconds, then rest in a chair, or better yet, go lie down.

Chapter 4
The Dancing, Laughing Wizard

This chapter holds the opportunity for you to step into an ongoing co-creative energetic dance with the Divine. Magical Awakening is more than just energy healing, and more than the *will-based* forms of magic as taught to many through books on Wicca, ceremonial magick, runes, etc. Once empowered to the first level of Magical Awakening your energy system will be gifted the ability to access several forms of Divine light, light that cannot be abused or misused, and yet which is always very playful, illuminating, and joyful. These forms of light have consciousness, and not only are hard-wired always to work for the highest good but also continuously work with the wizard healer to assist in awakening from the dream world we exist in. The system of healing that is offered through this book is based on the idea that we are here to play with the Divine, to laugh with God, Goddess, Merlin, Lady of the Lake. We are in this life to both enjoy it, be amazed by it, and experience the wonder of it, while simultaneously knowing that none of it is real, including ourselves. One thing I have noticed in my magical spiritual journey is that rigidity can defeat the journey, cause it to freeze, get stuck, and lose the aliveness of play. So, if all else fails, play with the energies you will learn in this chapter and others, for in doing so you are literally playing with God/Goddess, the Divine.

What follows soon is an empowerment to the first level of Magical Awakening. Your personal energy field will be upgraded with three Divine energy centers, one at the belly, which flows a light called Dragon Fire; one at the heart, which flows a light called the Grail; and one at the top of the head, which flows a light called Arthur's Crown. These three centers work collaboratively to help a person burn away negative energies, clear unwanted thoughts and memories, bring healing to our spiritual bodies, and, perhaps most importantly, remind us of our own playful Divine nature.

If you feel ready to embark upon this journey, pick a day when you will have plenty of time to integrate the empowerment. Normally I teach the first level of Magical Awakening as a half day class. Even though you can explore this book at your own pace, simply for receiving the empowerment you should set aside a time when you know you will not be disturbed for at least an hour. Most likely, you will want to explore your new energetic abilities once you have the empowerment, so also set aside additional time for yourself to play with and explore the new abilities you will have after the empowerment.

I recommend devoting half a day to learning the first level if possible, because as you work with the energies more and more possibilities are likely to unfold as your imagination engages this playful Divine form of energy. Meditate on when is the best day, the best time for you to engage the empowerment. And follow your intuition!

Know that the empowerment is also a healing. Your entire energy vibration is going to change to a higher level. That means you might find after the empowerment that certain situations, foods, and people that matched your energy vibration before the empowerment no longer feel in alignment with who you are. Think of it being like a caterpillar transforming into a butterfly, in that how you see yourself and how others see you is bound to change. You may find yourself drawn to new people, new foods, new life situations. And, you also might have to let go of things, people, and situations that no longer serve your highest good. That can include letting go of old emotional patterns, such as trying to please others or being less than honest with yourself about your true feelings. As these powerful shifts occur within your entire being, know that you are also being supported by the universe. If old emotions rise up that once were too challenging to confront, know that now you have the power to engage them, as well as tools to help transmute the roots of any suffering that they might cause you. Know as well that Merlin and Lady of the Lake are with you, and can offer additional healing magic to support this process.

They both work through the energies of the three cauldrons: Dragon Fire, the Grail, and Arthur's Crown, which you will have access to for the rest of your life after the empowerment.

Once you have meditated and arrived at the right day, the right time for you to receive the empowerment, do your part to make it a special day. You might want to wear certain attire that reflects the importance of this day. You may want to receive the empowerment at a location that feels powerful to you, such as near an ancient tree in the woods or in the proximity of the wonder of the ocean at the closest beach. Or you may wish to lie down in your own bed at a time when the full moon is casting its light through your window. If you want to be even more ceremonial about it, you can light a candle to Merlin and Lady of the Lake to show your gratitude for this gift. There are many ways one can show reverence and gratitude, and most likely you know what works best for you. But do something to mark this event as being a special moment in your life.

On the day of the empowerment, take a bath with a few pinches of sea salt in it to cleanse your aura. Or, if a bathtub isn't available, take a shower using sea salt wrapped in a small washcloth to cleanse your body. Sea salt and water is a wonderful combination for cleansing your aura. If you are choosing to wear any special attire, be meditative when changing into it. Treat it as though you are literally stepping into the cocoon from which you will emerge later as a magical butterfly. Also, know that the empowerment itself will be from this book, so bring this book with you to any desired location for receiving the empowerment.

Once all preparations have been made, make sure you have a place where you can comfortably lie down without being disturbed for an hour. Then, to engage the hour long healing empowerment simply touch the image of Merlin's magic book below, and allow the empowerment transmission to begin. Then let your finger go from the page, lie down, and receive the healing empowerment, which will run for approximately an hour. So, you wanted to be a wizard, and now you are!

Chapter 5
Playful Magic with the Three Cauldrons

Play is how we discover what our muscles can do, how loud our voices can be, how we communicate with our peers...at least that is what happens during childhood. We play, and learn how to walk, run, ride a bike, tickle, even our ability to use language grows through word games and rhymes. We learn so much by playing, especially when the grand scale of what we have to learn cannot always be put into a manual. Such is the case with being a wizard in the Magical Awakening lineage, the best way to learn is to play! Yes, there are some guidelines, but very few. For some, having that level of freedom to explore on their own can be uncomfortable. The preference for some is to have a strict guideline, a healing protocol. But if you deepen into the essence of play, of literally playing with the Divine through whimsical sacred energy, then an entirely new world will open for you where each second holds the possibility of wonder—and healing—to such a degree that the healing and wonder merge.

The sense of playing with the foundational energies of the universe, and knowing that sense of co-creating with the mystical forces of the Divine, that it is all good and that no harm can come from it, is exhilarating and mentally liberating. It allows a wizard to know that boredom is no longer an option, that none of life's moments are rote or mundane, that the being which created this universe is present within the energetic field of who we are as wizards. That in itself is a powerful transformation, an opening into a new way of thinking about life and the magical possibilities of becoming the magical life we always dreamed of. We do not live our future, rather we become it, filled with charm and wonder!

So let's begin playing with your new abilities, these Divine magical energy centers that have been woven into your energy field through the empowerment you received.

Begin by bringing your attention to the area of your navel. Know that from this moment forward you have access to an energy there called Dragon Fire. This Dragon Fire energy can burn away unwanted vibrations from all of your energy bodies, including your mental body, emotional body, chakras, as well as cleanse and purify the energy of a room, and more. Once you have brought your attention to the region of your navel, simply intend that Dragon Fire flow out now to your entire being into your entire physical body. Allow yourself to relax into this, with your consciousness directing the flow of Dragon Fire energy. You may experience this as a hot, fiery white light, or your experience may be more subtle.

Whatever your experience may be, know that Dragon Fire will flow simply by your intention. After sending Dragon Fire to your entire body, play with the energy, sending it to specific areas within your body. Below is a list of suggested organ systems, organs, and energy systems where you can send Dragon Fire for several minutes one at a time:

Brain and nervous system
Digestive system
Muscular system
Circulatory system
Respiratory system
Skeletal system
Lymph system
Liver
Kidneys
Eyes
Ears
Throat
Mouth and gums
Knees
Feet
Hands
Any area where there is an infection or weakness in the body
Chakras (either one chakra at a time or all at once)
Meridians
The gates of consciousness (two acupuncture points at the base of the skull)
Mental body
Emotional body

Etheric body
Karmic body

Allow yourself to play with the energy, for that is where your deepest level of learning will occur. That is how you will begin to form an intuitive relationship with the energy itself.

Now pick a certain life issue and ask that the Dragon Fire energy flow to wherever that issue is held in your entire being. It might be an old pocket of anger that is held in your liver, yet also in your chakras, meridiens, or one of your energetic bodies. Allow the Dragon Fire energy to flow continuously for several minutes. Again, notice any changes in your body, mind, and spirit as you do this.

Working and playing with the energy in this way teaches you that these "life issues" can have shape, texture, and sometimes many layers. As the shape of the issue begins to present itself, you can then begin to see it almost as a hologram of light, an energetic toy that you are playing with. The healing itself becomes a *game* of how you can shrink the issue until it completely disappears. And in this energetic play there is a knowing, and understanding, that this is all play, that these issues are all like shadow puppets we are simply trying to shine a light on until they disappear or change into something beautiful. This kind of play helps the wizard healer get out of the story behind the issue and just focus on the energy of the issue, which can have profound implications if completely transformed or released.

Having played with Dragon Fire energy for a while, now move your attention to the Grail energy cauldron at the center of your chest. For me, when tuning into this I literally see a magical grail cup in the center of my chest, which is likely just my visual interpretation of the energetic portal for how this light comes into my energy field from the Divine realms. But it looks like a grail, and there are many wonderful stories about the healing properties of the Holy Grail, so for simplicity I just refer to this light and this energy center as the Grail.

Begin by intending that light flow out from the rim of the cup, the Grail, and that it spin out through your entire body, all your energy bodies, your entire being. If you are energetically sensitive, you may notice that it has a different energetic quality than Dragon Fire does. The Grail light tends to be more soothing, nurturing, relaxing, restorative, balancing, and less about burning away negatives. Play with sending the Grail energy to specific systems one at a time within the body:

Brain and nervous system
Digestive system
Muscular system
Circulatory system
Respiratory system
Skeletal system
Lymph system
Liver
Kidneys
Eyes

Ears

Throat

Mouth and gums

Knees

Feet

Hands

Any area where there is a wound, trauma, or weakness in the body

Chakras (either one chakra at a time or all at once)

Meridians

The gates of consciousness (two acupuncture points at the base of the skull)

Mental body

Emotional body

Etheric body

Karmic body

Send to each of these for several minutes, and notice any sensations, any changes in your own consciousness that may occur. Notice how your energy bodies and organ systems interact with the energy of the Grail. Does it make you feel soothed, lighter, relaxed, nurtured, more balanced? When you send it to your emotional body, do you feel more calm? When you send it to your mental body, does it bring any awareness of ways you can improve your own ways of nurturing yourself? Again, just play with the energy, sending it where you feel intuitively drawn. Then, go deeper.

Try playing with sending the Grail into a specific issue, perhaps a time when you didn't feel nurtured enough as a child. All of this happens simply by your intention. Simply intend the energy to flow from the Grail, out through time to that time when you were a child. Be as specific and as detailed as you wish in terms of where you intend to send it on your own timeline of this life. The energy itself is not limited by time or space. Imagine sending this deeply nurturing Divine light to yourself at a time in the past when you may have felt alone, or simply misunderstood, unseen, or unloved. Continue sending the Grail energy to this issue for several minutes. Does it change your perception of that time in your life? Can you feel this Divine light impact you *then*? Continue sending this energy to various times in your life when you could have used additional nurturing, almost like you are playing tag with yourself through time. Keep it playful even if there are times in your life you decide to send it where you didn't feel playful at all. And, simply notice any changes in your consciousness, even if you do not entirely feel the energy itself, as not everyone will.

Having worked with the Grail energy thoroughly, bring your awareness up to the top of your head to engage the energy of Arthur's Crown. You may actually see an energetic golden crown on top of your head, as some wizards do when sensing this energy. This crown energetically represents us being connected to the Divine, and using that connection with grace and wisdom. Know that the energy of Arthur's Crown, more than any other energies in the Magical Awakening system, is about wisdom, and assists us in being the King or Queen of our own destiny as we use this sacred light to release the energetic obstacles that might hinder us manifesting our deepest purpose in life.

Once you have tuned in to the source of this energy at the top of your head, intend that it flow out through your entire being. Arthur's Crown works to literally awaken things energetically back into their own true Divine nature. As you send this wondrous light throughout your entire being, notice how it smooths out pockets of thoughts/emotions that may make you feel disconnected from your true Divine nature, like lifting the curtain in a dark room where there is a frightening shadow, only to see that sunlight is now bursting through the room. This Arthur's Crown energy, more than any other in Magical Awakening at this level, can bring about permanent change. It does so by awakening aspects of us energetically, back into that deep, ever-continuous connection with the Divine of our purest *be-ing*.

After sending Arthur's Crown to your entire being for several minutes, play with sending it to various organs, organ systems, and energy systems of the body just as you did with the Dragon Fire and Grail energies:

Brain and nervous system
Digestive system
Muscular system
Circulatory system
Respiratory system
Skeletal system
Lymph system

Liver
Kidneys
Eyes
Ears
Throat
Mouth and gums
Knees
Feet
Hands
Any area where there is an issue or trauma held in the body
Chakras (either one chakra at a time or all at once)
Meridians
The gates of consciousness (two acupuncture points at the base of the skull)
Mental body
Emotional body
Etheric body
Karmic body

Know that the purpose of sending Arthur's Crown to those systems is to literally awaken those aspects of your consciousness held in those systems that have succumbed to the dream that we are separate from the Divine. When those aspects of your mind awaken it is truly liberating! An intense dose of this energy to the brain and nervous system, as well as the mental body, can sometimes lead to one feeling complete bliss, a satori like state void of the mental chatter that often distracts us from being most completely who we truly are.

Perhaps one of the most powerful aspects of Magical Awakening happens when sending Arthur's Crown energy into your karmic body. Your karmic body is where all your karmic conditioning is stored. Think of it as the accumulation of thoughts and actions from this lifetime and others that can influence the opportunities and challenges that exist for you in this lifetime. If, for example, you have had a recurring issue of disappointing work situations lifetime after lifetime, then that energetic signature will exist in your karmic body, calling toward you similar events, similar patterns, as like attracts like. With Arthur's Crown you can send energy directly into the karmic body, and even focus on a specific life issue that is held in the karmic body. Often, Arthur's Crown will "wake up" the energetic signature that exists in the karmic body into realizing that it is actually an aspect of the Divine. As this energetic signature wakes up, it becomes emptiness, pure consciousness, and releases much of the drama that it has been creating for you lifetime after lifetime. Although not all karmic issues can be released energetically, many of them can be. Play with this, as if you were playing an energetic game of hide and go seek with the Divine. Send Arthur's Crown into your karmic body, to a specific issue, and see if it can awaken any of those energetic signatures enough so you begin to see their Divine presence, their Divine nature, and no longer be the captive of the Divine dreaming itself as something we call karma.

Try this for a number of minutes on one life issue as it exists in the karmic body. Send for several minutes, or until the energy of the life issue feels like it is becoming empty space. When it becomes empty space, know it has been awakened by the energy of Arthur's Crown.

Having played with Arthur's Crown energy, bring your attention back to the Grail for the final part of the magical healing. Imagine yourself in miniature, like a very small doll, sitting or lying down inside the Grail cup, inside the chalice. If visualizing this is challenging, simply intend that you are now inside the Grail. Simply by holding this visualization or intention, it activates a very powerful Divine light for integration.

This integration form of light energy helps you tie up any loose energetic threads, and helps you ground back into your physical being at the end of a session. You may experience a sense of fullness or pressure in the area of your chest as you perform this technique. That sensation is from you as the practitioner, and it is likely you will feel this sensation anytime you perform this integration technique on yourself, or others. At a certain point, several minutes into the integration, you will most likely feel a sense of completion, as though the Grail is so energetically full that no more energy can move for this session. When that occurs, simply give thanks to Merlin and Lady of the Lake for this wonderful magical gift. Relax. Drink some water. And know you can continue this form of energetic magical healing play anytime you wish.

Know as well that this energy healing outlined in the previous paragraphs is a *recommended* self-healing. As you work more with it over time, you are encouraged to adapt it as needed for any given issue or circumstance. The deeper you go into the Magical Awakening system, the more each individual wizard is encouraged to listen to their own intuition and inner guidance.

Chapter 6
Games of Magic

My years of teaching Magical Awakening have taught me that it is best learned through experience and development of the intuition of the practitioner. Unlike many other modalities of magic and healing, there is no rote formula, no strict one size fits all prescribed way for one to use it anymore than there is a prescribed way to have a conversation with a dear friend. It is a dance, of listening and playing, listening and playing. The childlike, playful quality of Magical Awakening helps the wizard healer in not taking themself too seriously, and thus helps a wizard cross that perilous bridge, the bridge of being effective and yet not self important. What follows in this chapter is a series of energy games a wizard healer can play. These games are designed to assist the wizard healer in understanding the energies of the three cauldrons of the Magical Awakening system, playing with them the way a child learns to engage the world that surrounds them originally through irreverence, being free, laughing, and finding what muscle does what...not by reading about them, but by running about and playing continuously!

Energy Game #1: Pick a room where you would like to brighten the energetic field, a room in a home, apartment, workplace, really any room at all. Just know that the larger the room, the more time you will need to thoroughly complete the instructions that follow. While in the room, intend that Dragon Fire flow out from the region of your navel. Intend that it flow across the entire floor of this room, along the walls, up around the entire ceiling. If there is furniture in the room also intend to send Dragon Fire to any furniture in the room. Simply intend that Dragon Fire is burning away any unwanted energies present in the room. Do this for several minutes, allowing your focus to be guided by your intuition. When you have finished, notice if the room now feels energetically brighter, lighter, more at peace.

Energy Game #2: Take a glass of water and taste it. Notice the energetic flavor of the water. Now, send Dragon Fire into the same glass of water for about a minute or two. Taste the water again, and see if you can tell the difference between the two energetic flavors. Now, send the Grail into the water, again for a minute or two. When you have finished, taste the water. Sense the energetic difference between the different tastes you have experienced. Now, send Arthur's Crown into the glass of water for a minute or two. When you have finished, taste the water as before. Notice and compare the subtle but often noticeable differences. Finally, imagine the glass of water inside of the Grail cup for integration. Allow this integration to go for a minute or two. Then, take a final sip of water, again noticing any difference. Know that we are mostly water, and these changes you experienced in taste happen through a person's entire body when you perform a Magical Awakening energy treatment on them.

Energy Game #3: Play energetic catch with Merlin! The way this game works is that whatever type of Magical Awakening energy you send into the hand below, Merlin will toss back to you a few seconds later. Try, and play for as long as you'd like.

Energy Game #4: Have a playful battle with the Dreadlock Octopus! The Dreadlock Octopus is a name I have given for the collected thoughts of humanity. These thoughts, though not at all bad necessarily, can be like a sludge that prevents us from directly experiencing our own reality. I imagine this being as a usually benign monster being made up of millions and billions of strands of thought, like little tiny hairs that reach through time from the head of everyone who has ever lived. In magic, thoughts are considered real things, not just personal experiences we have with our own minds. So, every thought that has ever happened, in the realm of magic, still exists. I call that culmination of human thought the Dreadlock Octopus! For this particular game, simply try to free yourself from the grip of the Dreadlock Octopus. In essence, such a feat is impossible, as our personalities, emotions, and social conditioning are deeply and irrevocably connected to other people's thoughts. Yet, in playing this game, it can help you discover more deeply who you are, and where your sense of self is connected to (or dependent upon) the thoughts of others. Also, you can create a wider range of personal freedom by learning where other people's thoughts and expectations sometimes take over and replace your own, without you even knowing it. A hint I have for battling the Dreadlock Octopus is to begin with those hairy strands of thought of the people closest to you. Do not send energy to clear those people, but to clear yourself of the influence of their thoughts. In the end, the only solution to co-existing with the Dreadlock Octopus is to learn to love it, like some unruly dog. Still, if you don't want that dog to rule your life, try playing this game frequently.

Chapter 7
Energetically Assisting Others with the Three Cauldrons

Magical Awakening is meant to be shared, and there are many ways it can be shared with others. Of the energy healing modalities I have been trained in, Magical Awakening gets the fastest and most permanent positive results, because it is designed for the Divine intelligence of the universe to move through you. This happens especially at the higher levels of Magical Awakening but also at the first level when a healing wizard has access only to the energy of the three cauldrons of Dragon Fire, the Grail, and Arthur's Crown.

Magical Awakening can be offered as either an individual session or in a group session format. Still, the technique is the same for both. If offering an individual session you would want to know something about the person you are working with. Begin by asking the person who is the intended recipient a few questions around their intentions of receiving the Magical Awakening treatment. It may be that they simply want to experience the wonder of this magical form of Divine energy healing, or they may have a specific life issue they would like you to address that exists on the mental, emotional, physical, or other level of their being such as in their karmic body. Usually a person will not know exactly where the issue is held in their being, but will know why they want change to happen in their life. Know to begin with that you are a wizard healer, not a psychotherapist, nor a medical doctor. You cannot legally diagnose, nor psychologically interpret for the recipient. Simply ask the recipient what they want you to address with the energy of Magical Awakening. Then let them speak. Listen attentively, again without interpreting or attempting to diagnose. Once you have been given the information that the recipient has been willing to share, ask them to lie down.

If you have a massage table for the recipient to lie down upon, that is helpful though not required. The recipient can lie down on a yoga mat, or a soft cushion such as a shiatsu mat. If you are sending the treatment distantly (as I prefer), the recipient can lie down on a couch or bed in the comfort of their own home. Though as a practitioner, one should never invite the recipient to receive a treatment on your own bed or coach, as that sends an inappropriate message that this might be something more than just an energy healing. During the treatment you do not need to touch the recipient and there is no need for them to undress as one would do in a massage. If you happen to be a professional bodyworker or energy healer, feel free to add any special touches to the experience such as relaxing music, aromatherapy, soft lighting, or any other creative techniques for making an ambiance most suitable for the recipient to relax and be at peace during the treatment.

Once the recipient is lying down and receptive, begin by listening deeply to the three cauldrons within your own energy system, Dragon Fire, the Grail, and Arthur's Crown. Usually, one of them will brighten or simply begin to flow energy on its own out to the recipient. I encourage you to listen to the energy, be moved by it as though you are an energy musician experiencing an energetic jazz improv session with the Divine. Again, there is no rote or specific manner in which the healing always must happen, as long as you perform integration at the end of the session. The key is in deep listening, as well as allowing yourself to be playful. What follows is a suggested routine if you find that you need it. Some people need a sense of structure the first few times they perform a healing, so a typical suggested session is provided below. Still, eventually the best way to work with the energy is to allow it to inform you moment to moment what energy to send, and where. Although a typical session is provided below, know that no healing, nor any person, nor you yourself are typical. In other words, it is simply a suggested session for those that want some structure, which you are free to ignore whenever the energy tells you to do so.

Start with Dragon Fire, allowing the energy to move through the recipient's entire system. Know that the energy itself has consciousness and wisdom and comes from the Divine. So, listen to it. Allow your mind to get out of the way and let this energetic dance come forth. Play with the energy, knowing that once it leaves the cauldron in your own energy system it will arrive wherever you intend it to go. Begin by intending this fiery hot white light called Dragon Fire move through the recipient's entire being, including the physical and energetic aspects, burning away anything negative, anything in their energy system not serving their highest good. Then, after several minutes, shift your focus to send Dragon Fire directly into the physical body. Keep playing with the energy, allowing it to flow from one system within the body to the next as you feel drawn or inspired. Send Dragon Fire to each system of the body one at a time for a period of minutes starting with the digestive system, then the brain and nervous system, then the muscular system, respiratory system, skeletal system, as well as all major glands and all major organs.

Once you have worked on all the physical systems in the body, begin sending Dragon Fire to the recipient's chakras, those seven energy centers that are essential to the Vedic systems of spiritual healing from India. Intend that it burn out any psychic debris that may be interfering with any of the recipient's chakras. Continue this for several minutes, then shift your intention to send Dragon Fire to the meridians, those energetic pathways through the body that are the core of acupuncture and Chinese medicine. You do not need to understand or be student of Chinese medicine to do this, as the energy you are sending is guided by the Divine and will do no harm. The energy will clear the meridians of any energetic obstacles, which once fully performed allows the meridians to function properly to promote optimum health within the body.

Now, once you have sent Dragon Fire into the meridians for several minutes, shift your intention again and focus Dragon Fire into the mental body to burn away any thought patterns that no longer serve the recipient's highest good. Play with this. You may feel the presence of projected thought patterns, conditioned responses learned from the recipient's family, friends, and teachers during childhood, which however well-intended may no longer serve their highest good. False beliefs, poor self-image, and other similar thought patterns can be diminished using this technique. After working on the mental body for several minutes, repeat the same process but now sending Dragon Fire into the etheric body for a few minutes. Then, follow with sending Dragon Fire into the emotional body, again for several minutes.

Once you have worked with Dragon Fire energy, then go ahead and move on to using the Grail. Begin sending energy from the Grail into the recipient's entire being for several minutes. Then focus your intention to send Grail energy into their physical body, focusing on one bodily system at a time. First, send to the digestive system for several minutes. Follow by sending Grail energy to the brain and nervous system, also for several minutes. Work through each system of their body one system at a time making sure that you devote several minutes to each: muscular system, respiratory system, circulatory system, and skeletal system. Conclude work on the physical body by sending Grail energy to all major organs and all major glands simultaneously for several minutes. Continue to play with this energy, sending it where you feel drawn and called, for as long as feels needed. Offer any special additional healing to areas that may be related to the issue named earlier by the recipient.

After working on the physical body, repeat the same process but now sending Grail energy into the mental body for a few minutes. Then, follow with sending Grail energy into the etheric body for several minutes and then the emotional body, again for several minutes.

Now, shift your intention to Arthur's Crown, sending this Divine light through the recipient's entire being, smoothing out any pockets of consciousness that are isolated from knowing they are interwoven with the Divine. Continue this for several minutes, then focus Arthur's Crown into the recipient's karmic body, again to smooth out and awaken any consciousness, any karmic patterns that are stuck and preventing the recipient from living a life of joy, freedom, and wonder. More than any other Magical Awakening tool at the first level, Arthur's Crown works well on releasing issues at the karmic level.

If the recipient gave you an issue to focus on, focus on its karmic root as you work on the karmic body. The way you can tell if you have fully released an issue in the karmic body is it will feel like the issue has turned into empty space, and the Arthur's Crown energy will simply flow into that void, that Buddha consciousness of pure emptiness some call nirvana or Divine bliss. Know that the recipient's life evolution may depend on some karmic issues remaining in place, so it isn't always possible to release a karmic issue just from your own desire to, it has to be ripe in the recipient's karmic body. Yet, there is no harm in trying to release such an issue. If it is meant to be released, it will be.

Now that you have sent energy from all three cauldrons it is time to bring the session to a close. Shift your intention back to the Grail, and simply imagine or intend the recipient in miniature, as if they were a small doll inside of the Grail. By doing this, you are enveloping their full being with the integrating light that comes from within the Grail. This light helps put everything back together energetically, helps ground the person back into an awareness of their body, and makes it less likely that there will be a healing crisis, even if part of the session helped release any major life obstacles or trauma. As you engage this process there will often be a sense of pressure or fullness in the region of your own chest. At a certain point, it will feel like the region of your own chest is so full of Divine light that no more energy can move. When this happens, know that the session has come to an end. Give thanks mentally to the recipient for this opportunity to offer them this healing. Give thanks to yourself for being a vessel of the Magical Awakening energy. Then give thanks to Merlin and

Lady of the Lake for bringing this wonderful healing energy back to humanity.

Once the session is complete, I usually will offer the recipient a glass of water and remind them to drink plenty of water for the next couple of days, which helps the kidneys to continue flushing out toxins released by the recipient during the session. If a distant session, simply remind them with an email or telephone call to drink plenty of water the next few days.

If offering a group healing to more than one individual simultaneously, which is a magical and wonderful aspect of this system, then simply repeat the above structure and intend the energy go to everyone in the room, or everyone in the healing if a distant healing that is nonlocal in space and time. It doesn't take any more energy or effort to work on twenty (or one hundred) people than it does one individual. The only difference is that the group healings have a more communal feeling if held in the same room, but the level of the healing is just as intense and just as complete. Group sessions that I offer to staff at Omega Institute are quite popular, and have had a noticeable, long-term positive impact both for those individuals who attend regularly as well as for the community as a whole.

Chapter 8
Enchantment of the Elements and Merlin's Wand

The following chapter offers the second-level wizard empowerment, which will open you to a deeper level of Magical Awakening. Once you have received the empowerment you will be able to access four elemental energies: the element of earth, element of air, element of fire, and element of water. These energies will come not out of the three cauldrons, but through your fingertips. You will also have an ability to call forth another energy from your fingertips, which I think of as a fifth element, called The Mists of Avalon. These mists that flow through the fingertips have but one purpose, which is to bring the recipient of the energy into a deeper sense of connection with Divine mystery. Also, you will have access to another energetic tool called Merlin's Wand, which broadens a wizard's ability to access the three cauldrons and elements simultaneously, with very little effort. Merlin's Wand is an energetic wand, not a physical one, and will exist in either hand, made available simply by your intention to use it.

A wizard's ability to access elemental energies through the fingertips is something that was explained to me once by my friend Marc Grossman, who is an eye doctor, co-author of the *Magic Eye 3D* book series, and yet also an acupuncturist. Once, when explaining to Marc about energy flowing from the fingertips in this manner, he told me that it made absolute sense, since there are acupuncture points at the end of each finger that act almost like energy transformers, which yin turns into yang and yang turns into yin. So, the idea that energy flows from our fingertips seems to already be happening, just that with the second-level wizard empowerment you will have an ability to call forth the energies of the four elements, as well as subsets of these elements. Let's look deeper at these four elements.

The element of earth corresponds with the physical body. This element, when called forth through the fingertips, can help relax and nourish one on the physical level. It can also be used to call forth any subset of the element of earth. A subset of the element of earth can be the energy of a particular gemstone, mineral, crystal, or even something in nature made of earth or of the earth such as a specific mountain, volcano, canyon, herb, tree, and more. When you think of the energetic subsets that are possible, just with this one element, the options are quite astounding and, for some, overwhelming to consider in terms of creating a specific protocol for any particular healing due to the vast number of variables one can manifest energetically through the fingertips. That is one of the beautiful things about this system, that it is designed to completely overwhelm the rational mind with so many possible options that the best path cannot be achieved through thinking, but must be arrived at through intuitive listening, engaging in an ongoing energetic dance with the Divine. This required intuitive dance continues to open the wizard healer, pulling them into a place of childlike play with the Divine where all becomes a whimsical energetic game.

The element of air corresponds with the mind, things related to thought, communication, writing, sounds. When calling this element through the fingertips it is very easy to bring a person into a calm and meditative state by stilling their mind, quieting their thoughts, which often helps allow the recipient to be more open to the healing as a whole. Some of the energetic subsets of the element of air can be animal sounds, wind, music, sacred sounds, and mantras, all of which can be very useful when offering a healing. Of all the elements used in Magical Awakening, I relate to this one the most and tend to use it more than the others, perhaps because astrologically I am an air sign.

The element of fire corresponds with a person's sense of will and creativity. It can also be used in ways similar to Dragon Fire to cleanse and burn out energies that are not for a person's highest good. However, the element of fire and Dragon Fire are quite different, which you can best learn by playing with both. Dragon Fire tends to flow stronger than its elementary counterpart. Yet the element of fire is more malleable and can offer a variety of subsets.

One subset of fire that I particularly enjoy working with is something I call angel fire, which flows through the fingertips and has a light, angelic quality to it that purifies but is far more gentle than using the basic element of fire, or Dragon Fire.

The element of water corresponds with the emotional body of a person, and can be used to bring a sense of deep serenity and inner peace that contributes to the gestalt of a Magical Awakening healing. Some of the subsets of water can include sacred springs such as the holy waters of Lourdes, or the Ganges River, or a sacred spring in Bali that I particularly enjoy working with called Tempak Sering. You can also call forth the specific energetic qualities of any of the oceans or lakes on the planet, each of which has its own energetic quality to it.

The Mists of Avalon, which I think of as the fifth element as I mentioned earlier, has one purpose, which is to take the recipient into a deeper connection with Divine mystery. Often, this enchantment sent through the fingertips can have a consciousness expanding or mind altering effect, in a way that is quite positive, allowing the recipient to remember themselves as beings of energy and spirit.

Merlin's Wand is an energetic wand that will exist in whichever hand you wish for it to be. It works to allow a wizard to access any energies you have learned so far in Magical Awakening with a simple flick of the wrist, as though you are shaking a real physical wand. This easy access also allows a wizard to create more play and many layers to a healing, creating a richness that is almost like an energetic symphony. How this is done will be explained more once you have the empowerment and can use this wonderful tool.

What follows in the next chapter is the empowerment for the second level on your wizard's path of healing magic. Yet for now, if you want to feel the elements in their basic energetic form, simply touch the appropriate symbol below. Know that once you are empowered to the second level of Magical Awakening, you will have an ability to shape each of these elements into subsets, such as a specific gemstone for the element of earth, or a specific sacred spring for the element of water, and so on. This ability is not one you will have by simply touching the elemental symbols below. They are there simply to allow you to feel these basic energetic forms for now, before your next empowerment, and also to inspire you to imagine the possibilities once you have engaged that empowerment. For now, play with touching these symbols. You can even try touching more than one symbol at a time to sense how their energies feel when combined:

Element of Earth

Element of Air

Element of Fire

Element of Water

There are no symbols for the Mists of Avalon or for Merlin's wand. To play with those energies you need to step into the following chapter, surrender your preconceptions, and let the laughter of the universe move through you.

Chapter 9
Laughing with the Elements, Dancing with the Wand

You have embarked on a journey, a journey of deep mystery and wisdom. Until now, you have explored many aspects of your own consciousness with the wizard tools of the three cauldrons. Hopefully, you have used your magic to better your life, improve your self worth, to uncover your true self. For some that might mean peeling away old traumas and wounds. For others it may be simply allowing their imaginations to sing. For most of us, it is some of both.

The playful qualities of Magical Awakening become vast at the end of this chapter when you receive the second empowerment. These qualities are so vast, it is hard to imagine and impossible to quantify. Let me give you an example of the kinds of things you will be able to do. You can use the element of air to bring your mind into deep stillness and inner peace, anytime, whenever you wish. Then at the same time use Merlin's Wand to layer in Dragon Fire energy into your mental body to burn out any thought patterns that do not serve your highest good. Then, flick your wrist again with Merlin's Wand, and while the two previous energies are still working, call in the cauldron of Arthur's Crown through the wand to awaken any aspects of your mind that are ready to awaken. All of this while simultaneously sending the Grail to nurture your physical brain and how it relates to the magic you are presently working. Then, wiggle your fingers to flow the element of earth as a subset energy of the crystal selenite to clear your mental body even more, all of this happening within a few short seconds at the start of a wizard self-healing. Imagine, and then know this is just one small possibility within a vast array of many. Imagine being able to engage such an energetic dance anytime you wish, be it alone in your room or walking in the park, or covertly among a crowd when feeling overwhelmed. There will be more exercises and games of play to teach you ways you can use the elements, and the wand. Yet for now, it is time to prepare for the empowerment that will grant you these energetic gifts.

Treat the day of the empowerment as a special one. Give it the same degree of importance as the first wizard empowerment if not more. Take into consideration where you wish to receive the empowerment, and when. Use your best wisdom to make this an auspicious day, be it on a full moon, the solstice, a sacred holiday, your birthday, or some other day that holds positive power in your psyche. Once you have chosen the day, give thought to your attire, making any necessary wardrobe arrangements that will add to the quality of your experience, whether than means wearing all white, a robe, or being skyclad (nude), even adorning yourself with sacred jewelry. Allow your own intuition and your own self-expression to guide this process. There is no one correct way, other than to be yourself. Give thought as to whether you wish to add ceremony to the empowerment, such as lighting a candle to Merlin and Lady of the Lake on that day. Be creative in thinking how you may want such a ceremony to be. Remember, we are all part of the Divine, all sacred in our own way. You don't need to do it any other way than the way that feels special to you.

On the day of the empowerment, do something to clean yourself energetically, such as taking a sea salt bath, or smudging your aura with white sage. You might even consider sending a prolonged Dragon Fire self-healing to cleanse and burn out any negative or unwanted energies. Know that as you do this you are preparing yourself for the next stage on your wizard's journey. When you have finished cleansing yourself, step meditatively into your attire, whatever that attire might be as long as it feels special to you. Also, know that the empowerment itself will be from this book, so bring this book with you to any desired location for receiving the empowerment.

Once all preparations have been made, make sure you have a place where you can comfortably lie down without being disturbed for an hour. Then, to engage the hour long healing empowerment simply touch the image of Merlin's magic book below, and allow the empowerment transmission to begin. Then let your finger go from the page, lie down, and receive the healing empowerment, which will run for approximately an hour.

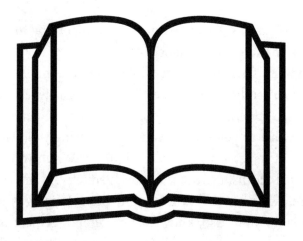

Chapter 10
Playing with the Element of Earth

Mastering the elements takes a long time. Unlike working with the three cauldrons, each element has almost infinite possibilities when a wizard considers the vast number of subsets and combinations of subsets within each element that can apply to uplifting and bringing positive light to any given situation. So, let's take it slow for the next few chapters, focusing on one element at a time before bringing them all together with Merlin's wand and the Mists of Avalon for a deeper magical healing.

Know that the way to activate an elemental energy to flow is by simply wiggling your fingers and holding a specific intention related to which element, or elemental subset, you wish to have flow from your fingertips. This action is something I call an enchantment of the elements, as it brings forth the energy of the element, or subset of an element, mixed with your intention. Try this now, pointing your fingers on both hands toward you, wiggling them for a few seconds, and intending that the element of earth flow out to you. At first do this without any specific intention other than it be the element of earth that is energetically flowing from your fingertips. Then, after these few seconds, simply shift your thoughts so that the element of earth now has an intention given to it. Intend that this element, which rules things on the physical level, assist your body in feeling relaxed. Keep using the element of earth to relax your physical body, changing your focus now from your entire body to specific muscles or regions of the body where you might feel tension. Continue playing with this for a short time, as you don't want your fingers themselves to be overworked or feel tired, which is possible for those who are constantly accessing elemental energies in this way. When you are done wiggling your fingers, simply notice how you feel. Do you feel more relaxed or less stress in certain areas of your body?

Another technique I like to use with the element of earth, one that is particularly useful at the end of a session, is to energetically create a grounding cord using the element of earth. A grounding cord is often mentioned in certain schools of psychic study and energy healing, and can often be created by an individual through visualizing a cord or tube of light coming from their root chakra at the base of the spine and going all the way down to the center of the Earth. Some might sense this cord as an energetic tether that reminds us that we are made of Earth, and are part of Earth, something that often is easy to forget in our Western-based culture, which gives too much emphasis on the mind and often ignores the body. Creating a grounding cord for yourself or another using Magical Awakening helps keep a person connected to the Earth at the end of a session. If you have ever experienced a deep energy healing that left you ungrounded, you will know the benefit of creating a grounding cord. Grounding cords help keep a person stable and centered after a healing. Try creating a grounding cord for yourself now using the element of earth. Simply point your fingers toward yourself and wiggle them with the intention that you are creating an enchantment of the element of earth to manifest a grounding cord from the base of your tailbone all the way down to the center of the Earth. Do this for approximately thirty seconds, then allow your fingers to rest. Notice how you feel after creating the grounding cord. Do you feel more connected to the ground? Do you feel more present in your body? Simply notice what you feel, and know you can create a grounding cord anytime you feel as if your are getting lost in your thoughts, or as if you aren't really present in your body. Grounding cords can be useful many times during the day and do not have to be limited to being used in a full-blown Magical Awakening session.

Let's focus now on creating subsets of the element of earth. A subset of the element of earth can be anything that is made of earth such as a mountain or landscape, or anything that is composed of minerals such as plants and trees. Try now using the element of earth to call forth a subset of this element as the energy of a particular landscape on the planet, hopefully someplace that you feel connected to. It can be a hill, mountain, valley, an area of forest or desert. Know that you can use this same technique to call forth the energy of a place you haven't been, but for our playful experiment it is best to start with places you know. Point your fingers toward yourself and wiggle them with the intention to bring in the energy of a familiar landscape that is pleasant to you, which could be a park you played in as a child, a hill that you used to climb, or other similar landscape. Notice how it feels in your body after wiggling your fingers for even just a few seconds. Is there an energetic presence coming from your fingertips that reminds you of this particular landscape? Does this energy invoke any kind of resonance in the cells of your body? In other words, does it make you happy, alive, curious, solitary, or some other sensation?

Remember, landscapes have huge impacts on our being. In ancient Greece doctors would prescribe geographic remedies to cure illness. And anyone who has known the majestic feeling of being at the top of a mountain can certainly understand the possibilities that can unfold by energetically calling forth a similar presence. Keep playing with the possibilities, wiggling your fingers and intending the energies of various landscapes to come forth. Once you have played with calling forth the energetic presence of landscapes you are familiar with, then move on to try some you do not know. Play with calling forth the energy of the Grand Canyon in Arizona, Mount Everest in Nepal, the volcano Gunung Agung from the island of Bali, or the jungles of the Amazon rainforest. Notice how all of these feel to you, how they make your body feel when calling these energies forth from your fingertips. Know that although you may call forth a landscape that can create a feeling of discomfort (such as an energetic sense of the deep cold of Antarctica) you cannot do any harm. Nothing in the Magical Awakening system can harm. It can only be used for good, and any attempt to misuse it for harm simply results in the energy not flowing at all. That being said, sometimes a landscape might be less appealing than another, and as with any form of energy healing sometimes we need energies that will bring an issue to the surface for a deeper healing. In any given situation, as long as you are listening deeply to your inner guidance and the energy itself, you will know what energies to call forth.

Once you have exhausted a sense of playing with the possibilities of landscapes as subsets of the element of earth, try working with the energies of various plants, including trees. Wiggle your fingers and call forth the energy of the herb chamomile as a subset of the element of earth. See how it feels to you energetically. Notice any sensations in your body. Then move on to try another herb, such as arnica, wiggling your fingers again to call forth this herb in energetic form through your fingertips. If you happen to have some wisdom about herbal remedies, then feel free to try different herbal combinations. But do not get lost in your thoughts. Remember, it is by the wizard healer engaging in deep intuitive listening that Magical Awakening is most effective. Listen, and feel if there are energies of specific plants that want to come forth from your fingertips. Try working with trees as well, such as the giant redwood, the sturdy oak, or the weeping willow. What energies resonate with you the most? Just notice, and be aware of any changes in your psyche and body as you continue to play and explore.

Now, after resting your fingers for a little bit, begin again. Wiggle them now to call in the element of earth as a subset of that element in the form of the crystal selenite, which is a wonderful crystal for clearing away negative energy. As you wiggle your fingers, pointing them toward yourself, intend that this selenite energy move through your entire aura and energy field to clear away and release anything negative, anything not serving your highest good. Do this for a minute or two, then rest your fingers and simply notice how you feel. Do you feel more clear energetically? Are there any cluttering sensations you had before in your thoughts or emotions that now are no longer there? Just notice what you feel.

Keep playing with the element of earth, finding different subsets of that element as stones, crystals, landscapes, herbs, trees, and more. You literally have the world now at your fingertips, so take the time to learn all the many healing vibrations that can be held in stones, mountains, trees, and more. Sometimes, a wizard will hear intuitively something that may make no rational sense at all. For example, once a wonderful student of mine was performing a healing on me and decided to flow the energy of the volcanoes of Hawaii to me. It had a huge heart-opening impact, a sense of deep love that I never would have imagined. Similarly, it wasn't something she premeditated ahead of time. She was simply told by her guides during the session to send me the energy of these volcanoes. That is the way Magical Awakening works. There are almost infinite possibilities. And you will learn to listen to them, even if they don't make the most rational sense. A similar healing I had from another student of mine involved this student running the energy of an ancient stone. The stone wasn't something you would find in a book on the healing properties of crystals and gemstones. But the student listened anyway to what Merlin and Lady of the Lake were telling him. It ended up that the stone held a deep understanding of the flow of time, and this way of bringing the stone energy through for the healing amplified both the students and my own sense of time, which was what was needed for the healing. So, you cannot always predict exactly how something is going to work. Just trust that it will, and keep listening and playing with the Divine, using the energy at your fingertips as an amazing and wonderful way to embrace your connection to all that is.

Know that the above exercises are just a small few of the vast number of possible options one can explore with this one element. Make a practice of playing with the energy daily, trying new subsets of the element of earth, to discover to as many possibilities as you can. You will discover some that will become your favorites. And some may come through only once but will make that one healing extremely magical. If you want to practice working with this element and its many varied subsets of possibility, just go back to Game #3 in Chapter 6 of this book and play energy catch with Merlin, but now using your knowledge of the element of earth as well as the three cauldrons.

Chapter 11
Amusing Yourself with the Element of Air

The element of air is the one that I prefer to use the most in my exploration of Magical Awakening possibilities. It isn't that it is better than the other elements, or more useful. It is simply that I am an air sign and so often relate to things more from that quality of air, thought, communication. One thing I love about the element of air is how quickly it can change a wizard's mental state, or the recipient's mental state, when used with intelligence. Try this exercise, which is one I use in almost every Magical Awakening healing I do: Access the element of air in its basic form, not using any subsets of it, to simply bring your own mental body into a place of deep stillness and inner peace. To do this, just point your fingers toward yourself and begin wiggling them while holding this intention of bringing your mental body into a place of deep stillness and inner peace. Try this for just thirty seconds or less, and often in that time alone you can create a profound shift in your mental state. Notice if you feel more still, more quiet, as if the thoughts have been wiped off the canvass of your mind and all is spacious serenity.

Try another similar experiment, again using only the element of air in its basic form, without any subsets. With this experiment the invitation is simply to bring your consciousness into the present eternal moment. Do this by simply holding that intention, wiggling your fingers while pointing them toward you, to bring in the element of air and allow it to manifest your intention. Try this for about thirty seconds, then allow yourself to notice anything new or different, as if you now can fall into those spaces between each thought. Notice your mind, if it is chattering endlessly as minds so often do, or if it is in a place of deep unity with all that surrounds you.

A favorite technique of mine using this element is to focus on an issue held in the mental body as a particular negative way of thinking or negative self-image, then wiggle your fingers to call forth the element of air in its basic form intending that it concentrate and bring to the surface this thought pattern entirely. Once you feel like the negative thought pattern is completely out in the open, then send Arthur's Crown energy into it to literally "wake it up." What happens when you wake up a negative mental pattern in this way is that the energy of which that pattern is composed is awakened into remembering its own Divine nature, and the thought pattern itself simply turns into emptiness, as though it has reached nirvana and no longer holds you hostage.

Try this on yourself now. Pick a thought pattern you have that no longer serves your highest good. It can be something as simply as a pattern of worry, a pattern of seeing yourself as less than whole, or some similar thought pattern you wish to move beyond. Now, wiggle your fingers, pointing them toward yourself, and intend that you are bringing all aspects of this thought pattern out into the open and up to the surface. When doing this, you may feel discomfort because the thought pattern will be very clear in your awareness. Once you sense the pattern is fully out in the open, then shift your intention and begin sending Arthur's Crown into it from the cauldron at the top of your head. Continue sending this energy until it feels like Arthur's Crown is simply going into empty space. When this occurs, know that you have awakened all of the pattern that is ready to be awakened. Sometimes it may take repeated effort to fully release all the layers a pattern may have. But for now, notice how you feel. Does it feel like that thought pattern has less control over you? It may be that the pattern is entirely gone, and you no longer sense it inside of you. Use this technique whenever consumed by thoughts that you feel are not serving your highest good.

Now, let's try a different enchantment of the element of air, again using just the basic elemental form without going into a specific subset of that element. Try an enchantment of the element of air to assist you in communicating with a non-human, sentient being. This can be an animal or plant, though all things have some degree of consciousness, even manmade machines. But for now, let's stay with those beings that we can more easily communicate with. To do this exercise you will need to go outside, unless you have a house pet or house plant that is available. Once you have identified what it is that you wish to communicate deeper with, make sure you are nearby it in physical proximity. If it is a dog for example, make sure you can see the dog and the dog can see you. Similarly, if it is a bird or a cat, make sure you can see it, and that it can see you if it wishes to. If using a plant to communicate with, make sure you can see the plant. Now, having identified and standing in proximity of that being, wiggle your fingers, pointing at the space between you and the animal or plant, intending that the element of air is working to enhance communication between the two of you. As you do this, try to be conscious of not allowing your subconscious mind to add in any grand ideas, which the subconscious mind can sometimes do. If you think your dog or cat or plant is suddenly telling you to go play the lottery, or that you are the reincarnation of Napoleon, then most likely that is just your subconscious mind playing with you. But if the animal or plant is simply sharing information that is curious, and perhaps useful in a practical way, then most likely that is a more real communication you are experiencing with the animal or plant. Often, the kinds of responses I get from animals may be things like the animal telling me it is hungry, or unhappy, or elated, or sharing an idea with me about some way I can improve my own life. These suggestions tend to be practical, not over the top. Similarly, when working this kind of enchantment with the plant world you may get a sense if a plant needs water, needs to be moved, or is filtering out negative energy from an area in your home or near your home. Again, the messages from the plant world, as with the animal world, will often be as practical if not more so than your communication with a human being.

Try this enchantment several times, each time with a different animal or plant, just to practice how it feels. This enchantment does require a certain degree of openness, an ability to witness all beings as worthy of our attention. So, if that feels like too much of a stretch, I recommend not engaging this particular enchantment of the element of air until you feel curious and open to the possibilities. If you go into it assuming it won't work, then it won't simply because your own mind isn't open. That would be like trying to make a telephone call with a phone that has been disconnected. Instead, the analogy I like to use is this technique works more like boosting the cell phone range of a cell phone that already works, and is willing to take incoming calls no matter what the source.

Now, let's try working with some subsets of the element of air. One subset of the element of air I enjoy working with is sacred mantras and sacred healing sounds. The beauty of this is that you don't even necessarily need to know the exact sound of the sacred mantra. For example, I often will use an enchantment element of air to call forth Merlin's sacred healing chant. It isn't a healing chant I have ever actually heard before, unless that was from the time I heard him speaking to me in Gaelic. But, I know it exists. And as long as I know it exists, it can be accessed energetically. Try this yourself now by pointing your fingers toward yourself and wiggling them to call forth Merlin's sacred healing chant as a subset of the element of air. You may feel things happen in your body that you do not expect. Sometimes when doing this, I feel the vertebra in my spine loosen as though I was receiving an adjustment by a chiropractor. Sometimes I feel my thoughts lighten and brighten. Sometimes I simply feel a very penetrating light move into each cell of my body. I don't always know what is going to happen, but I do know it is going to be good for me. So, do your best to trust and surrender when doing this exercise. Try it for a minute or so, then let go of wiggling your fingers and simply allow yourself to be in the energy of Merlin's sacred healing chant.

Another subset of the element of air I enjoy calling forth is music. Often, I will access the energetic aspect of a wonderful piece of classical music to help calm a person's energy, or even to calm the energy in an entire room. One of my favorite pieces to call upon is Bach's Air. Know that when recreating music energetically it isn't that one normally hears the actual music as much as one feels the sensation that that music tends to invoke. Try this now, pointing your fingers toward yourself and wiggling them with the intent to call forth the energy of a familiar song that is pleasant to you. Keep wiggling your fingers for about thirty seconds or so, and then simply allow yourself to be in the vibration you have called forth energetically. Try playing with this possibility for the next few minutes, calling forth a familiar song, sitting in the vibration of it, and then moving on to a different song to see how it feels. Do you notice them? Do you feel an energetic difference between the different songs? Which ones make you feel inspired, or happy, or relaxed? Come to know and understand these songs that can now move through your fingertips are literally elixirs of sound that can heal.

The above techniques are just a few of the options one can use to work with the element of air. Again, the element of air rules the realm of the mind, including communication, words, as well as vibrations that move through air such as sounds and music. Know that in allowing your imagination to roam free, you will often arrive at wonderful magical options that may seem outside the normal box of an energy healer's repertoire, such as calling upon the element of air to recreate the energy of a gentle wind to clear the stuffiness of a room, and so on. Below are suggestion options you can try playing with to feel their effect on your energy system: Hebrew names of God from the Kabbalah, Indian Vedic mantras, Tibetan mantras, any sacred chant or inspirational song, the poetry of Rumi, sacred scripture such as the 23rd Psalm from the Bible or the Buddhist Diamond Sutra. The list is endless, and these are just a few wonderful places to start. If you want to practice working with this element and its many varied subsets of possibility, just go back to Game #3 in Chapter 6 of this book and play energy catch with Merlin, but now using your knowledge of the element of air and the element of earth as well as the three cauldrons. Enjoy playing catch with the great wizard!

Chapter 12
Lighting Up Your Life with the Element of Fire

This may be the only book about healing that encourages you to play with fire. Of course I am not talking about the tangible, physical fire you can create by lighting a match, but its energetic counterpart that can be accessed in ways that are completely benevolent through using the Magical Awakening technique called enchantment of the elements. Fire itself tends to enchant, which you will know if you have ever stared into a fireplace as a child or focused on a candle flame when meditating. Fire is mysterious, transformative. And playing with this element can truly help create fast and wonderful changes in your life.

To begin with, let's access the element of fire in its basic form, just to see what it feels like in our own energy system. As with the other elements, you can access it by pointing your fingers toward yourself and wiggling them with the intention that you are calling forth the element of fire. Do this now just to notice how this element feels in your energy system. Once you have wiggled your fingers to create the enchantment of this element for about thirty seconds, then let your hands and fingers rest while you allow yourself to be in the energy of fire. Notice how it makes you feel. Do you feel energized? Do you feel creative? Do you feel inspired? These are just some of the attributes of fire, but listen deeply to your own sense of what being in this energetic fire does for you. It is always very possible that your own experience will not fit the suggested possibilities. Know they are just suggestions, and the real truth of your experience should be what your experience is, uncensored, without having to conform to what this book might suggest.

Once you have played with fire the first time, now play with it again but with a deeper intention. Point your fingers toward yourself now, and wiggle them as you did before to create an enchantment of the element of fire. But this time intend that this fire cleanse your energy system. Keep wiggling your fingers for about thirty seconds, and then rest in the fiery energy you have called forth. Notice how it makes you feel. Do you feel lighter? Do you feel more clear? Know that this method of energetic cleansing can be very useful, and yet is not a replacement for using the cauldron energy of Dragon Fire, which tends to flow stronger and deeper than its elementary counterpart. My experience is that the element of fire works faster, but doesn't go as deep. Try playing with both and see yourself what the results are in your own energy system.

Now, try playing with the element of fire again in its basic form, but with a different intention. Point your fingers toward yourself and wiggle them to bring on the enchantment of this element. This time, intend that the fire energy is energizing you, making your muscles and organs feel more awake and alive. Do this for thirty seconds, and then simply allow yourself to be in the enchantment of fire once it has been created. What do you notice? Allow yourself to take inventory of any sensations that might seem fresh or new. Then, for the sake of playing, play with fire again, this time holding a different intention that it help focus and empower your will related to a project you might have in your own life, whether that project is about getting more exercise, writing a book, finding a new job, whatever it may be. Simply call forth the element of fire in its basic form to focus and strengthen your will, using the method of wiggling your fingers to bring the energy of fire through your fingertips. Then, notice how you feel about that project in your own life that you want to focus on. Know that this simple technique can be a gateway to keeping yourself motivated and focused.

Let's now try working with some subsets of the element of fire. These subsets are ones that I particularly enjoy using, but also feel free to discover your own after reading this chapter, again allowing your inner guidance and imagination to take the lead. Right now, try an enchantment of the element of fire as the Burning of Zazobra. The Burning of Zazobra is a ceremony well over a few hundred years old that takes place annually in Santa

Fe, New Mexico and involves much music and dancing, then setting fire to a huge puppet that represents Old Man Gloom. I often think of it as the original burning man, as the whole town gathers in a huge celebration to burn away their troubles, sorrows, bad luck, and more. Simply point your fingers toward yourself, intending to call forth the energy of the fires that burn Zazobra, then wiggle your fingers and allow the energy to move out from your fingertips into your energy field. Do this for approximately thirty seconds, then notice how you feel afterwards. Then, repeat the entire exercise again, but having a specific worry or sorrow in mind that you wish for this fire to consume.

Another subset of the element of fire I enjoy working with are the ceremonial flames of the Hindu aarti ritual. Aarti is a Hindu ritual of purification and blessing that involves wicks that are soaked in ghee (clarified butter) held within the aarti lamp, which is then moved in circles around a the image of a deity, and it is said that the flame then embodies the energy of the Divine. The ritual itself can be quite beautiful to witness and participate in, but for the purpose of Magical Awakening all you need to know is that the aarti flame purifies.

Try using an enchantment of the element of fire as an aarti flame to purify your own energy field. Again, begin by pointing your fingers toward yourself and wiggling them with the intention that the energy of an aarti flame come forth. Often, I point my fingers toward my head when doing this since in the traditional aarti ritual one would motion their cupped hands near the flame, as if capturing its light and bathing the top of their head with that light. Try performing this enchantment of the element of fire as an aarti flame for about thirty seconds. Then, allow yourself to be immersed in that light. Notice any changes in your consciousness. Do you feel more clear, more open, more aware?

Play with the element of fire using the above suggested options, and also create some of your own, such as calling forth the flame from the candles on a birthday cake during one of your happiest birthdays. Try it, and see how it feels. As is always the case, listen to your own inner guidance and intuition. And don't be afraid to play. Continue practicing with this element and its many varied subsets of possibility by going back to Game #3 in Chapter 6 of this book and play energy catch with Merlin. Except now use your knowledge of the elements of fire, air, and earth as well as the three cauldrons. Enjoy playing catch as your mastery of these elements continues to grow.

Chapter 13
Swimming in the Element of Water

The element of water rules the emotional body as well as the subconscious. Using this element as an enchantment in Magical Awakening can be a powerful way to move through energetic blockages in the emotional body. A dear friend of mine whom I work with using Magical Awakening said that after only a few sessions she was able to move past emotional issues that she had been struggling with for fifteen years in therapy. After a few sessions those issues were gone for her.

Let's begin by playing with this element in its basic form, without using any subset of this element. Start by pointing your fingers toward yourself, then wiggling them as you have been when calling forth enchantments of the other elements. Simply allow this energetic form of the element of water to bathe over you for about thirty seconds. Then, allow your hands to drop and your fingers to rest. What do you notice about the energy you have called forth? What kind of shifts happen in your awareness?

Having simply experienced the element of water without a specific intention, let's now give shape to your experience by having a focus for the energy. Intend as you are wiggling your fingers and pointing them toward yourself that you are calling forth an enchantment of the element of water to bring your emotional body into a place of deep serenity. Simply keep wiggling your fingers for about thirty seconds as you hold this intention of bringing your emotional body into a place of deep serenity. After approximately thirty seconds, allow your hands to drop and your fingers to relax. Notice what you feel. Do your emotions feel more peaceful than before? Do you feel serene? Scan your feelings to see what is going on for you emotionally. Often when I use this technique I can shift from feeling upset or chaotic into being centered, calm, and at peace. It is a great technique to use both at the start and at the end of a session.

A favorite technique of mine using this element is to focus on an emotional issue, then wiggle your fingers to call forth the element of water in its basic form, intending that it concentrate and bring to the surface this emotional issue entirely. Once you feel like the issue is completely out in the open, then send Arthur's Crown energy into it to literally "wake it up." What happens when you wake up an issue in this way is that the energy of which that issue is composed is awakened into remembering its own Divine nature, and the issue itself simply turns into emptiness, as though the issue itself has reached nirvana and no longer holds you hostage. Try this for yourself. Pick an emotional issue you have, then use the element of water to bring it entirely to the surface simply by wiggling your fingers and intending that the element of water is bringing that issue to the surface in your emotional body. Then, once it feels the issue is fully out in the open, send Arthur's Crown from the cauldron at the top of your head to wake it up. When it reaches a point where Arthur's Crown feels like it is flowing into empty space as opposed to the issue, that is when you know the issue itself has awaken ed, that the energy it is composed of has returned to that Divine void. This technique can be very useful for moving though emotional challenges. Use it whenever you need to.

Now, let's play with specific subsets of the element of water. Use enchantment of the element of water to call forth waters that you already have a connection to, be it a specific pond, stream, lake, river, sea, or ocean. Just point your fingertips toward yourself and wiggle them, intending that this specific subset of the element of water energetically flow forth from your fingertips. Try this for thirty seconds, and notice any energetic shifts it creates for you. Then, try another subset of the element of water, again using one that you are already familiar with, be it a beach you have visited, a lake you have gone swimming in, or a waterfall that inspires you with awe. Just wiggle your fingers while they are pointed toward you, intending that the energy of this specific subset of water flow forth as an enchantment. Keep playing with this several times over, each time trying a different body of water as the subset. When you are finished, note the different qualities each subset of water manifested in your energy field. Be aware of how you feel, as sometimes water can calm and other times it can stir things up for a deeper healing.

Having played with water in these subsets, now try playing with an enchantment of the element of water as Niagara Falls, flowing through all of your chakras to cleanse them of any energy not serving your highest good. Keep wiggling your fingers in the usual manner for creating an enchantment of the elements, all the while intending that this enchantment is to bring the energy of Niagara Falls rushing through your chakras from top to bottom. Do this for thirty seconds. Then, notice how you feel. Be aware of your thoughts, your emotions, and any unusual sensations.

Having played with the above options, continue to play, for that is how we best learn. And, it allows our egos to be more malleable, more fluid. The goal in Magical Awakening isn't to dissolve the ego, but simply to awaken it into a place of magic and play.

Now, let's try another enchantment of the element of water. Point your fingers toward yourself and intend that the enchantment of the element of water come through as Holy Water. This can be the water blessed by the hugging saint and avatar known as Amma, the water of the Ganges river, the water of Tempak Sering, the holy healing waters of Lourdes, the holy water in the basin of a local church, or any water that has been blessed or is said to hold special healing powers. Allow your fingers to wiggle to call forth the enchantment for at least thirty seconds, though you can go longer if you wish. Once you feel ready to bring it to an end, simply let your hands drop, your fingers rest, and allow your consciousness to be aware of any shifts in your energy. Continue to energetically swim in this element, playing with its many varied subsets of possibility by going back to Game #3 in Chapter 6 of this book and playing energetic catch with Merlin. Now you can use your knowledge of and access to all the elements, as well as the three cauldrons. Know that practicing playing with these energies is the only way to truly understand them. So, play with the wizard, dance with the Divine, and see what unfolds in your consciousness as you do so.

Chapter 14
The Mists of Avalon

I often think of the Mists of Avalon as a fifth element, the element that brings all the others together and reminds us of the never-ending mystery of the Divine. There are no subsets for the Mists of Avalon, nothing to invoke other than its pure form. To me, it truly feels like a mist, a spray of soft Divine light that is almost intoxicating with the joy of falling deep into the mysterious arms of the Divine. To use Mists of Avalon simply point your fingers toward yourself and begin wiggling them, as you do when creating the other elemental enchantments. I tend to do this for about thirty seconds, then let my fingers and hands rest while I enjoy being immersed in the elegant mist of Divine light.

Mists of Avalon is wonderful to use at the start and end of a session, whether working on yourself, another individual, or a large group. It constantly reminds of that deep mystery of the Divine, that we can touch, and yet never quite fully explain. It is this mystery that for me is part of the joy, this sense of going deep into something, knowing you will never quite fully know all of it. For some, that may be intellectually challenging, especially for those who are fact driven in their approach to life. But I feel it more like a Divine teaser, something that keeps me wanting to delve deeper into my spiritual practice, deeper into my magic, simply because I fully understand that there is always something more to discover, something new that will be shown to me.

Try playing catch with Merlin using Mists of Avalon. It is truly a joyful experience. Go back to Game #3 in Chapter 6 of this book and play. Try focusing on just this one energy, instead of adding other elements as suggested at the end of previous chapters. Just play, and see what magic unfolds.

Chapter 15
Merlin's Wand

Merlin's Wand is an energetic wand, not a physical one. It will exist in whichever hand you intend for it to be. It is the true essence of a wizard's magic, in the sense that it is invisible, can shift from one hand to the other, and yet has the ability to access almost anything in the Magical Awakening system. At higher levels there are a few tools beyond what this book explores that it cannot access, but for the most part all of the Magical Awakening system can be accessed through Merlin's Wand. It will give the wizard access through the wand all tools at that level of Magical Awakening that the wizard is empowered to. On the surface, that might not seem like such a big deal. If the wizard is already empowered to those tools, how does Merlin's Wand help? It helps by almost being like a secondary healer, one that can be accessed with the flick of a wrist, guided with the wizard's intention.

Try playing with Merlin's Wand now to learn how it works. Begin by simply intending which hand the wand will be in, either your left hand or right hand. Once you have decided, use the wand to begin sending yourself some Dragon Fire energy. This can be done simply by shaking the invisible wand toward yourself a couple of times, while simultaneously intending that it send you the energy of Dragon Fire. With just a couple of quick shakes of the wand, the energy will begin to flow. Usually, if you intend a specific number of minutes that you want the energy to flow, it will flow for that specific amount of time. Try this again, now. Shake Merlin's Wand a few times in your direction and intend that it send Dragon Fire to you for the next five minutes. Then let yourself simply relax into the energy. You may notice that although Dragon Fire is flowing through your system it isn't coming from the cauldron at your belly. Notice it is coming from an outside presence of Merlin and Lady of the Lake, yet this is energy that you can now access through the wand.

Let's try another playful experiment. Use Merlin's Wand to send yourself some energy of the Grail. Again, do this with a few shakes of the invisible wand in your direction. Usually anywhere from one to three shakes is enough. It doesn't take much, just bit of intention and a flick of the wrist. Allow yourself to relax into the Grail energy after you have invoked it through the wand. If you need for any reason to end the flow of energy, simply shake the wand again in your direction intending that the energy stop flowing.

Now, let's access Arthur's Crown through the wand. As before, just shake the wand toward yourself a couple of times, intending that it send you some Arthur's Crown energy. After a couple of shakes of the wand, let yourself simply relax into the energy. If you want the energy to stop flowing for any reason, just shake the wand again intending that the energy stop flowing.

You can see now that Merlin's Wand gives you access to all the energies of the three cauldrons. This is helpful because you can now send multiple layers of energy at once. Although it is possible to do this without the wand, sending energy simultaneously from more than one cauldron at a time can be challenging in terms of a wizard maintaining their focus on all three cauldrons simultaneously. With Merlin's Wand, you can simply shake the wand at yourself or whomever is the intended recipient, first intending that it flow the energy of Dragon Fire, the Grail, or Arthur's Crown. Then, once that initial energy is engaged and flowing, you can follow with another layer of energy by shaking the wand again. Try this now on yourself. Begin by shaking Merlin's Wand to invoke the energy of Dragon Fire to flow for the next five minutes through the meridiens of your body. Then, immediately, once you have finished invoking the energy of Dragon Fire by using the wand, follow with a few more shakes of the wand to invoke the energy of the Grail to flow through the emotional body for five minutes. Then, immediately after that, shake the wand again intending that it flow Arthur's Crown into the karmic body for five minutes. Then simply relax into the energies that are flowing to you, accessed by the wand. After the five minutes comes to an end, you can use Merlin's Wand to put yourself into the Grail for integration. Go ahead and do this once the five minute session has drawn to a close.

Merlin's Wand can also access any of the elements. So, this adds even more abilities for a wizard to layer in a multi-energetic level of healing at any given time. Below are a few suggested energy recipes you can try on yourself, just to see how they feel. Remember too, you can always adjust these energy recipes to fit you own personal need, or simply to try it a different way and give validation to your own magical curiosity. These few are just to inspire you to play with ways that Magical Awakening can be used, and are not intended to be rules written in stone for those wizards unwilling to listen deeply in the moment and respond simply to the energy itself, which is always the preferred method.

ENERGY RECIPE #1 FOR GENERAL WELL BEING

Shake Merlin's Wand to invoke Dragon Fire to purge out anything negative for five minutes
Simultaneously add the Grail to the brain and nervous system for five minutes
Toss in Mists of Avalon for thirty seconds
Add element of air to bring the mental body into deep stillness and inner peace
Add element of water to bring the emotional body into deep serenity
After the initial five minutes, shake Merlin's Wand to bring Arthur's Crown into the karmic body
Add element of fire as angel fire to the chakras

Add element of fire to focus the personal will for highest Divine purpose

Close with integration inside the Grail, using either Merlin's Wand or the Grail cauldron

ENERGY RECIPE #2 FOR SPIRITUAL CLARITY

Use Merlin's Wand to invoke Dragon Fire to clear all illusion from the mental body for five minutes

Simultaneously add Arthur's Crown to clear emotional blindspots for five minutes

Add Mists of Avalon for thirty seconds

Add enchantment of the element of earth as selenite to clear negative entities and untrue thought forms

Add enchantment of the element of fire as angel fire to continue deep clearing of anything untrue

Add enchantment of the element of fire as aarti ritual to purify your consciousness

Use cauldron at top of the head to send Arthur's Crown directly into any question you have (this connects your consciousness with the question...so best not to use Merlin's Wand at this point)

Add element of air simultaneously to bring stillness in listening to the answer

Close with integration inside the Grail, using either Merlin's Wand or the Grail cauldron

ENERGY RECIPE #3 FOR STRESS RELEASE

Begin with enchantment of the element of air to bring mind into stillness and inner peace
Add enchantment of the element of water to bring emotional body into serenity
Add enchantment of the element of earth to relax the physical body
Add enchantment of the element of fire as angel fire for cleansing the energy bodies
Use Merlin's Wand to send the Grail to relax entire nervous system for ten minutes
Simultaneously use Merlin's Wand to send Dragon Fire to burn out all energetic sources of stress for ten minutes
Add Arthur's Crown after ten minutes to smooth out the mental and emotional bodies
Sprinkle Mists of Avalon as needed throughout
Close with integration inside the Grail, using either Merlin's Wand or the Grail cauldron

Try now creating some of your own recipes, knowing that the best chefs and the best wizards often need no recipe at all. But it is in using recipes that we learn what our ingredients (magical or otherwise) do. Now, go play catch with Merlin using all of the Magical Awakening tools you have learned so far. Go back to Game #3 in Chapter 6 of this book and play, play, play. Try focusing on different layering techniques, different combinations of energy. See how they feel in your system as Merlin throws them back to you. Make sure you use not just the wand, but also the three cauldrons, and keep on wiggling your fingers!

Chapter 16
The Typical Session

I often encourage my students to discover their own path with Magical Awakening. Although I give pointers to what is possible, I always think the best teacher for any student is the energy itself. That being said, as one entirely new to the system it is good to have at least a framework for what a typical session would be. This framework is the same whether you are sending Magical Awakening to yourself, another individual, or a group. Know that as one gets into higher levels of Magical Awakening, the script for a session becomes less and less routine and relies more heavily on the practitioner's own intuition and guidance. Below is a rough outline for offering a typical session:

Start the session by using any of the relaxing/clearing enchantment of the elements such as angel fire (fire), chakra clearing (fire), bringing mind into stillness and peace (air), bringing serenity to emotional body (water), physical relaxation (earth), or gemstone properties... but make sure you know the property of the gemstone energy you call forth (earth). This normally takes one to five minutes depending on how many enchantments are used. Listen to your intuition as you are creating these enchantments. Sometimes only one is needed. Other times, a combination is better. Listen to your intuition and play.

Once you have invoked the initial enchantments of the elements, bring your attention to the cauldron at your belly and send Dragon Fire for ten minutes through the entire system to warm the system and prepare it for deeper work, also intend to clear away and burn out any negative energy (thought forms/anything harmful/etc.).

After you have sent Dragon Fire for approximately ten minutes, then call forth a specific issue, using an appropriate elemental enchantment (water for emotions, air for mental patterns and mental conditioning, earth for physical body, fire for anything related to will/purpose), it takes only a minute or two. Use your wiggling fingers to literally bring that issue (whatever it may be) to the surface and out into the open. Then send Arthur's Crown into the issue to awaken it back into Divine Oneness. Allow approximately ten minutes for this cycle to complete. If you feel that the issue has released before the ten minutes, then ask Arthur's Crown to work on the karmic root of the issue for the remainder of that allotted time.

Once you have finished working on this issue, then shift to sending the Grail on the entire system to help the mind/body/spirit know itself as whole and Divine for approximately seven minutes.

Afterwards, use the inside of the Grail for integration, approximately five minutes but may vary depending on depth of the healing and ability of the person's energy system to integrate.

Ending options use any combination of the following: use Mists of Avalon to take the person deeper into Divine Mystery; use Earth enchantment on person for self-love of the body; use Air enchantment to bring mind into the absolute present; use Water enchantment to call forth internal bath/holy spring or waterfall for purification and refreshing the whole energy system; use Fire to awaken person to their own Divine will.

Grounding/Energizing: Use enchantment of the element of earth intending it for grounding the person (or people) being worked on, and a Fire enchantment for energizing as the final two aspects of any session.

This typical session offers much room for improvisation and even encourages it. Know that at all times you should listen to the energy itself. Let it guide you. Let it speak to you. In this deep place of listening you will come to possible ways of using the energy in any given specific session that I as the author of this book cannot predict. Just know that those amazing possibilities are there.

Chapter 17
Developing a Daily Practice

Magic is contagious! And it makes life beautiful and wondrous. At least that is this wizard's opinion. I love being able to change the energy of a room to make it more positive, help a friend who is feeling ill, or release my own deep traumas from the past. I also love being able to communicate more deeply with nature using the element of air, feel the energy of a whale song come through my fingertips, or summon an ancient healing mantra from a language I don't understand, yet feel the profound effect of it anyway. I am a wizard, through and through. But I also notice and realize that for some it takes effort to engage magic as a daily practice.

Being taught for years (or centuries if you believe in past lives) that magic isn't real, or that it must be evil if it is real, has certainly shaped the consciousness of our modern society. When I was on tour for my first energy healing book *The Reiki Magic Guide To Self Attunement* (Crossing Press 2007), I sometimes would get very hostile comments from confrontational Reiki practitioners in the audience who demanded I explain why I used the word magic in the title of the book. I explained that for me energy healing of any kind brought forth a deep renewed sense of magic, like the magic wonder of a child. Although my explanation was true, and repeated many times over, it made me question on a deeper level why did this question keep coming up, especially among an audience of Reiki practitioners who are taught to change the energy of a person's being by using symbols and chants...what can be more magical than that? And yet these same people were attacking me for using the word magic, as if it was something evil.

Magic is part of our birthright. For me, it is part of the joy of being human. And yet there is a huge stigma in our culture against magic. Scientists dismiss it as irrational, and therefore we question the sanity of anyone who believes in it. Also, and perhaps deeper, for hundreds of years the Catholic church tortured and killed people who believed in magic as so-called witches. Those burning times were a holocaust that killed millions of people over hundreds of years, a slaughtering of herbalists, midwives, and those pagans who believed in the healing power of nature and magic. That group fear of being killed for believing in magic still exists in the collective Western psyche, and is something any wizard needs to eventually grapple with.

The best way to overcome it is to practice magic daily, make a routine of it. You can also make a practice to shift any negative thought patterns about magic that might be held in your mental body or any old emotional fears about magic held in the emotional body. To do this, use the element of air to bring to the surface any negative thought patterns about magic held in your mental body, then use Arthur's Crown to wake them up. What will happen is that literally the energy of which those thought patterns are comprised awaken back into their true nature, returning to a kind of nirvana and thus losing any negative charge about magic. Similarly, confront any fears about magic by bringing them to the surface in the emotional body, using the element of water to bring them to the surface. Then, wake them up using Arthur's Crown. They too will return to a kind of nirvana and lose any negative charge about magic.

Another way to own your new wizard abilities is to exercise them any chance you get. One way to practice this is shift the energy at home or work to a more positive vibration anytime you wish. Here are some options you can try for making that happen: Use the element of fire as angel fire to cleanse the walls, floor, ceiling of a room, including any furniture; send Dragon Fire into the space of a room; use the element of air to pull to the surface any negative thought patterns that might be existing in a space, then use Arthur's Crown to wake them up; send the element of earth as the crystal selenite into the space, walls and ceiling of a room. Know you can do any of these with discretion if need be. Try playing with just these few options, just to discover how it feels in a space when doing them. Does it make it feel brighter, clearer, more alive?

Other ways to practice using Magical Awakening daily are to do short treatments on yourself when you wake up and also when you go to bed. Each morning, when you first wake up, allow time for you to perform the Typical Session, knowing you can vary from it as you wish. Then each night before you go to bed, perform Energy recipe #3 to help you relax and release any stress before going to sleep.

Also, use your imagination as much as possible. If you want to experience dolphin songs, use the element of air (which rules sound) to invoke them. If you want to know the healing properties of a certain crystal, call it forth as the element of earth and feel what it does for you energetically. Really, a wizard's imagination is the key. I can only point to possibilities, but the real magic is within you. As you use Magical Awakening more and more, your own life will begin to feel more magical.

Chapter 18
Excalibur and The Magical Jewels of The Grail

Magical Awakening is a system of spiritual energy healing with eight levels taught to the general public, and then a ninth teacher level that is by invitation only. You have explored the first two levels in the previous chapters. Now, let's look at the tools of the third level of Magical Awakening.

The third level of Magical Awakening involves activating two new tools: Excalibur and The Magical Jewels of The Grail. At first glance, it would seem like the addition of just two more tools wouldn't comprise a whole other level for a Magical Awakening wizard. But these tools are quite strong and deepen what a wizard can do in ways that warrant this being a separate level of wizard training.

Excalibur is an energetic sword of light. Once you are empowered to the third level of Magical Awakening, you will have access to this sword. It can destroy negative energy faster than anything else in Magical Awakening at this level. It can also reach deep into the karmic body to transform and clear issues at their root. Once you receive the empowerment in the following chapter, this sword will exist about six inches in front of the line of your chakras. The handle of Excalibur will be about six inches in front of your root chakra. And the sharp tip of Excalibur will exist about six inches in front of your crown chakra. You will also be able to energetically access the sword through Merlin's Wand, if you prefer. The power of this sword can be used for healing, releasing negative energy, and also for psychic protection when needed. The way it is used is you simply imagine inside of Excalibur whomever or whatever you are wanting to send Excalibur energy to. Remember, Excalibur is a sword of light. So, imagining someone or something inside of that light can be very easy. If you do feel it is challenging however, you can always use Merlin's Wand to send Excalibur energy as well.

Just to let you know the versatility and power of this tool, I once used Excalibur at a full moon ritual event where a manipulative facilitator who was invited to lead a portion of the event was trying to steer a captive yet innocent audience to invoke some darker and malevolent forces. As one who has studied magic for over two decades, I was well aware of the negative potential of the energies this person was trying to get the whole room of a few hundred people to invoke. Yet, this facilitator was in true command of the stage. So, I simply remained in the audience and imagined all the psychic manipulation that was happening going into Excalibur and being annihilated. As the facilitator continued to attempt their misguided work, I could see the growing sense of frustration on her face that these negative beings she was attempting to invoke were not showing up. The room was remaining psychically neutral, with no real presence of these beings she was manipulating the audience to call in. I did nothing to harm her or anyone else, for Excalibur cannot be used to harm, only to defend. But, the success of Excalibur in this instance showed me not only its power for fending off any negative kind of psychic energy, but also made me wonder how deep this same power can go for releasing deep karmic issues from the karmic body given how powerful Excalibur showed itself to be in this instance.

Once you are empowered with Excalibur you will be given more specific exercises to use it. But for now, know that it is activated simply by imagining a person or other intended recipient inside of the sword. This activates the sword to then send its light to that person or other intended recipient. Again, know that the sword cannot do harm to someone. Still, I would not put someone inside the sword without their consent. Even in the case of the manipulative facilitator, I did not put her into the sword but simply envisioned anything manipulative that she was energetically sending into the room being destroyed by Excalibur. Neither the facilitator, nor anyone in that room, was ever actually sent any Excalibur energy. The energy was sent simply to protect the space from the manipulative psychic forces that the facilitator was trying to call in. In essence, Excalibur was simply protecting the space, and not allowing anything negative to come in.

Excalibur energy has a very yang overpowering vibration to it. If you need to get something done, in many cases this is the tool to use. And it doesn't take long to get results. However, Magical Awakening is a system of balance between male and female, yin and yang. And the other tools you have access to at this level are the Magical Jewels of the Grail, which are quite yin in their expression, quite spacious, recalibrative, and rebalancing energies as opposed to the fierce, overpowering energy vibration of Excalibur.

The Magical Jewels of the Grail are not actually jewels in the energetic sense. They simply appear as jewels. When a wizard wants to use them, they will magically appear on the surface of the Grail. These jewels however are actually bubbles of Divine consciousness, spacious bubbles of emptiness that you as a third level Magical Awakening wizard can put anything into, be it a person, a person's organs, a relationship, a situation, even your own path as a Magical Awakening wizard. Like Excalibur, once you have imagined the person or other intended recipient into one of these jewels it will activate the Magical Jewels of the Grail energy to be sent to them. The impact is much more subtle than when using Excalibur, but do not mistake this gentleness with being ineffective. The Magical Jewels of The Grail can energetically open one up in profound ways, offering balance, nurturing, and a deep recalibration to the highest purpose and highest level of healing.

These two tools often work in great harmony together. One can use the Magical Jewels of the Grail to open a person's energy system, which then allows Excalibur to dive in for the deep removal of anything negative that needs to be released. Exercises exploring this technique will be shown to you once you receive the third level wizard empowerment in the following chapter.

Know as well that once empowered at the third level both of these tools will also be available to you through Merlin's Wand.

Chapter 19
Becoming A Sovereign Wizard

The tools you engage at the third level of Magical Awakening open your magical abilities to release so much conditioning from your karmic body, as well as other energetic life obstacles, that you truly become sovereign of your own destiny, you become a Sovereign Wizard. Arthurian legend tells us it was because Arthur claimed Excalibur that he became king. So it is true that when a wizard claims their own sword of light, their own Excalibur, they too become the king of queen of their own life.

At the end of this chapter exists the option for you to step forward as a sovereign of your own destiny, to claim the sword of light known as Excalibur, as well as the Magical Jewels of the Grail. As with the previous two empowerments, you will want to prepare for this sacred occasion. Pick a day that holds a special meaning to you. Wear attire that feels fitting of the occasion. Cleanse yourself before the empowerment by taking a sea salt bath or sending a prolonged Dragon Fire session to yourself. Do whatever you need to do to make it feel special to you. If you want to create an altar with candles, write a poem or song to mark this day as special and sacred to you, then do so. As before, know that the empowerment itself will be from this book, so bring this book with you to any desired location for receiving the empowerment.

Once all preparations have been made, make sure you have a place where you can comfortably lie down without being disturbed for an hour. Then, to engage the hour long healing empowerment, simply touch the image of Merlin's magic book below and allow the empowerment transmission to begin. Then let your finger go from the page, lie down, and receive the healing empowerment, which will run for approximately an hour. This is the largest of Merlin's books so far, because the magic it holds is more powerful and deep.

Chapter 20
Embracing Excalibur

Excalibur is a sword of light that runs adjacent the lines of your chakras, with the handle at the area about six inches in front of your root chakra and the tip about six inches in front of your crown chakra. I used to think it was kind of like a collective of all the power in all of the chakras, acting as one unified field. I no longer think that, especially since investigating more and more of the Magical Awakening levels teaches me that all the tools and systems in Magical Awakening come from the Divine. They can be downloaded into our energy system, but are not dependent on our energy system for their power, since that power comes from a Divine source. Excalibur is a sword of light that protects against negative energy and can also help release issues at their deepest core, cutting away at their roots.

Let's begin using Excalibur to sense and feel how awesome its potential feels in your own energy system. Excalibur first presented itself to me a few months before

I knew about Merlin's Wand. So, originally the only way to access it was to imagine whomever or whatever you are sending energy to as if it were inside the sword. And though I think it is still important to work with that original technique because it brings a level of energetic connection to the sword that otherwise does not evolve, for now let's access Excalibur through Merlin's Wand, simply because it is easier and allows you to focus more in the sensations in your body that happen when you are receiving a healing from Excalibur. Later in this chapter we will use the original technique.

Now, simply bring your attention to Merlin's Wand and shake it toward yourself a few times very quickly, intending that it invoke the energy of Excalibur to run on your karmic body. Do this now, then relax for a few minutes while receiving the short energy healing from Excalibur. You may notice some sensations in the area of your spine, since much karmic conditioning is held in that region of the body. What do you notice? Are the sensations strong? If they feel too strong, simply wave Merlin's Wand and ask that the session come to an end. Otherwise, relax into the sensations for the next few minutes until they come to an end.

Now, let's work with Excalibur again but with more of a focused intention. Again you will be sending Excalibur into the karmic body, but this time pick an issue in your life and intend that Excalibur work to help root out that issue at the deepest level. The issue can be an issue at work, something to do with relationships, finances, health, your connection to the Divine, anything at all that you feel could use some improvement. Once you have identified the issue, shake Merlin's Wand a couple of times toward yourself, intending that Excalibur work on the intended issue. Usually a few quick flicks of the wrist to shake Merlin's Wand is all that is needed to get the energy flowing from Excalibur, though you may add more if you feel a desire or need to. Pay attention to any images or sensations that might arise as the energy is flowing. If you need to adjust the healing, bring in any enchantments of the elements or the three cauldrons, then do so. But, since this is just a sample healing for the purpose of demonstrating how Excalibur works, try your best to keep the healing to just a few minutes.

Once when using Excalibur to work on a karmic issue related to success I sensed the presence of another person who was part of the larger equation of this karmic issue. And my guidance told me that this other person was blocking my success to a certain degree in a way that was not at all conscious but was based on old karmic conditioning between me and that person. So, in this healing I invoked Excalibur several more times to not only address the larger issue I was working on, but also on the direct karmic conditioning between me and this other person. Only after working to heal the karma between me and this other person was I able to get the overall energy to shift for the better. So, again, it is always important for the healer wizard to go into a place of deep inner listening when working with Magical Awakening.

Now, let's try Excalibur again, still accessing it through Merlin's Wand. Think of a time in your childhood when you felt bullied or mistreated, whether by another child or an adult, maybe even a teacher or school principal. Then access Excalibur by shaking Merlin's Wand several times, intending that Merlin's Wand annihilate any negative energy that was sent to you at that specific point in time, any negative energy from verbal abuse, teasing, or any other negatives you would like to release. Since this is using Excalibur to send energy distantly in time and space, feel free to give the wand a few more shakes than usual if need be. It isn't that it requires more effort to send healing distantly in time and space, but that sometimes it is harder for us performing the healing to notice the changes as quickly. Again, this is in part due to the disbelief many people have in the ability to use magic at all. So, if more energy will help you to notice the effects, then feel free to add the extra effort to make that happen. Once you have sent what feels to you like enough shakes of Merlin's Wand, then relax into the healing. Notice any sensations, memories, emotions that may arise.

When I send energy backwards in time, whether through Magical Awakening or other forms of energy healing such as Reiki, it isn't that I think I can change the past. No one can change the past. But what we can change is our reaction to the past. Often, our reaction to a past trauma is heavily influenced on energetic cords that still exist to another person in the situation who was abusive, or unexpressed emotions that have been held inside for years. By sending healing energy into the past you don't change the events of the past, but you can change how the energetic vibration of those events still influences you today, you can change their energetic signature. I have spent many hours in my own personal healing sending energy into the past, and have felt the profound positive effects of doing so.

Next on our journey using Excalibur, begin by sending its energy to your mental body. Identify a thought pattern that you may have that isn't helping you. Once you have identified that pattern, use Merlin's Wand to call forth Excalibur to annihilate that pattern. When you annihilate a thought pattern with Excalibur, the energy of that thought pattern simply returns to pure light.

Notice how easy and simple it is to use Merlin's Wand to invoke Excalibur. Know that that ease can help create even deeper layered healings that will be explored in later chapters. But for now, let's try the original technique for using Excalibur, which is a little more challenging but helps you to build a deeper connection with this amazing sword of light.

Imagine that you can see Excalibur about six inches in front of the line of your chakras, with the handle in front of your root chakra and the tip of this sword of light in front of your crown chakra. I normally see Excalibur as made out of a golden light, but some may see it as made out of a silver light or a white light as well. Even if you are not well inclined to visualization, simply intend that Excalibur is there. Now, imagine or intend that you are inside of this sword of light. As you hold your focus on this sword, imagining or intending that you are inside of it, it activates the energy of Excalibur to flow out through your entire being. Allow this to happen, all the while still imagining or intending that you yourself are inside of this sword of light. Notice how it feels.

Some may find it challenging to both hold the intention of being inside the sword while also feeling its powerful energetic presence. But, if you can, hold this image of yourself inside the sword for as long as possible. Notice again how it feels to your body, this intense energy moving through you that annihilates anything that might be harmful to you. Once you feel as if you have had a full experience of Excalibur energy, which often can be just a few minutes, then relax and let go of visualizing yourself inside of the sword of light. Then if need be, put yourself into the Grail for integration, as often just a few minutes of Excalibur is enough of an energetic shift to warrant using the Grail for integration. When you feel fully integrated, write about what you felt, what you experienced. It is by documenting the effect of Excalibur that you will come to fully understand it as the amazing and powerful tool that it is.

Excalibur can be used for clearing karmic issues, offering psychic protection, and clearing away negative energies and negative entities. It is one of the tools I almost always use in Magical Awakening sessions. In later chapters, you will learn how to use it in combination with the other tools you have learned so far for a deep layering Magical

Awakening healing treatment. But for now go practice tossing swords with the great wizard! Just go back to Game #3 in Chapter 6 of this book and play energy catch with Merlin, but now using your knowledge of Excalibur.

Chapter 21
Exploring Divine Consciousness Through the Magical Jewels of the Grail

The Magical Jewels of the Grail are one of the more mysterious tools in Magical Awakening. They exist on the outside of the Grail and can be thought of as bubbles of Divine consciousness that are part of the Grail, which shift and change like the quarks and charms of quantum physics, leading to a certain unpredictable magic in the work they do. Often, they change from one session to the next, and can even change during the individual treatment. You may see diamonds, rubies, sapphires, or other gemstones surrounding the outside of the Grail at any given moment. Know that whatever needs to appear for the healing involved will appear at that given time. Working with Magical Awakening at this level is entirely about surrendering the issue to the Divine, as again there is not a predictable focus or intent you can hold when working at this level. Simply surrender and imagine the person you are working on inside one (or more) of the Jewels.

This level of healing requires a deep level of surrender to the Divine, and yet can work on issues at a multidimensional level, releasing the thought forms and inter-dimensional issues that often feed or cause our life dramas in ways far beyond psychologically rooted problems or life issues. Uses for the Magical Jewels of the Grail can include seeing or visualizing various individuals within separate jewels for a group, relationship, or family healing or seeing various organs or organ systems within various jewels, holding them there for balancing and clearing, while also working on how these organs relate to and inter-depend upon each other. Also, though often many jewels will be present on the surface of the Grail, you may be called to work with just one, or even just a few. Let your intuition guide you in this work. Trust that these bubbles of Divine consciousness know what to do. More than any tool you have used so far, this one is entirely about surrender and trust in the Divine as a practitioner.

At times it may seem hard to clearly identify exactly what the Magical Jewels of the Grail are doing in a session, though usually there is a kind of energetic rebalancing and recalibration that occurs. Still, it is in this place of surrendering it to the Divine that something deeper happens with this tool that is beyond words, beyond a mind's ability to comprehend and give language to. The Magical Jewels of the Grail will appear on the outside of the surface of the Grail, often in irregular patterns, with various jewels showing themselves. Once the jewels reveal themselves, allow your consciousness to be guided to one of them. Then imagine or intend that whomever or whatever you are sending energy to is inside the jewel. The jewels themselves are really nothing more than bubbles of Divine consciousness, but they present themselves as jewels. What can be more of a precious jewel than a condensed bubble of Divine consciousness anyway?

It is important to note this as a wizard, as some students of mine have become confused into thinking that when they want to send the energy of a particular real-life jewel, such as a ruby or sapphire, they should try to use Magical Jewels of the Grail, when in fact they should use an enchantment of the element of earth of those particular jewels that they wish to invoke the energetic quality of. Remember, the Magical Jewels of the Grail are bubbles of Divine consciousness that visually sparkle and illuminate. They can appear in different colors and different shades of color. They look like jewels, and Merlin and Lady of the Lake refer to them as jewels. But in reality, they do not invoke the energy of any particular jewel and are simply bubbles of Divine consciousness with their own kind of magic.

Try accessing them now just to see how they work. Simply intend that the Magical Jewels of the Grail appear on the surface of the Grail. Once they do, allow your consciousness to be guided to one of them. Usually many of them will appear, but normally only one of them will call to be used in a session. When you have intuitively identified which jewel is calling to you, intend that you are putting yourself into that jewel, allowing yourself to exist inside this bubble of Divine consciousness. (If you are someone who does see these Magical Jewels of the Grail when you ask them to appear, simply hold a strong intention that you are inside of one, even if you cannot see it, and that will get the same result.) Do this now and see what it feels like. Allow yourself to relax into whatever this bubble of Divine consciousness has in store for you. Do you feel more spaciousness when inside one of the Magical Jewels of the Grail? Do you feel calm, a sense of peace? Do you sense your energy shifting and changing in subtle but noticeable ways?

Notice whatever it is that you feel during the few short moments after putting yourself into one of the Magical Jewels of the Grail. Then, try playing with them at a deeper level. Again ask them to appear on the surface of the Grail and allow your consciousness to be drawn to one of them. This time, intend that you are putting your liver inside of the jewel that has called to you. Notice how the area of your liver feels to you in the short moments after intending or imagining it is inside one of the jewels. Does it feel like it is being energetically rebalanced? Does it feel more peaceful, more expansive, more calm? Now, try to examine the Magical Jewels of the Grail that are still present on the surface of the Grail while your liver is still intended or imagined to be inside one of them. Allow your consciousness to be called now to another jewel, and this time intend that your stomach is inside of that jewel. Again, notice any sensations around your stomach as you do this. Continue visualizing these jewels on the surface of the Grail, imagining or intending that specific organs are inside each one. Every time you do this, allow yourself to take note of any sensations, any feelings, any emotions that arise. Then after playing with this for a while and working with whichever organs you feel drawn to put into these jewels, you can let go of this exercise and simply notice how you feel overall. Do these organs feel more balanced, more calm?

What I sense happens when putting a person or organ inside one of these jewels is that it is like reconnecting them with the original source, that Divine spaciousness as a mode of consciousness, like the Buddhist nirvana, the empty space of bliss of no-thing. It is as if the form itself is reminded that it comes from formlessness. And in that interplay between form and formlessness, healing happens, inner peace arises, rebalancing occurs.

Now, try again working with the Magical Jewels of the Grail, but this time using Merlin's Wand. When using Merlin's Wand it is much easier to access these jewels and takes less concentration, thus making it easier to focus on the results of the healing as opposed to the process of the healing. Still, sometimes it is good to use the technique of visualizing the jewels on the surface of the Grail instead of using Merlin's wand, as that helps you develop a deeper and more conscious connection to the Magical Jewels of the Grail. Eventually, you will learn to use both simultaneously for even deeper layered healings.

But for now, just shake Merlin's Wand toward yourself a few times, intending that it is putting all of your major organs inside one of the Magical Jewels of the Grail, so that each organ is inside a different jewel. Then, once you have invoked that with a couple flicks of your wrist, shake Merlin's wand again and intend that each vertebra of your spine is inside its own jewel. Then, give one more shake of Merlin's wand, intending to put your whole body inside of one jewel. Now, just relax. Relax into the spaciousness around each organ, around each vertebra. Allow that Divine void within to rise up and be felt, be seen, and to rebalance your entire being.

If you would like to continue playing with this new tool, work with putting a situation or a relationship into one of these jewels. Try this now by shaking Merlin's Wand a few times and intending that you are putting some challenging relationships into various jewels. Know that in doing this you are not sending energy directly to anyone else, but more changing and rebalancing the energetic ambiance of the space shared between you and that person. Once you have invoked the Magical Jewels of the Grail through Merlin's Wand, and intended a few challenging relationships into those jewels, simply relax and surrender to the healing. After a few minutes, notice if your feelings about any of those relationships has changed. Do any of them feel lighter, more at peace? Sometimes you may even have an insight, a key to bringing that relationship into a place of Divine harmony. Know that this technique, if you use nothing else in Magical Awakening, can be a key for opening doors to a happier life, greater success, and healthier relationships both in your career and personal life.

Know that the above exercises are just a small few of the vast number of possible options one can explore with the Magical Jewels of the Grail. Make a practice of playing with the energy daily, putting your organs, organ systems, relationships, situations, and as many possibilities as you can into the Magical Jewels of the Grail. You will discover some techniques that will become your favorites. And some may be important through one time only healings that are extremely magical. If you want to practice working with the Magical Jewels of the Grail and its many varied possibilities just go back to Game #3 in Chapter 6 of this book and play energy catch with Merlin, but now using your knowledge of all the tools in the first three levels of Magical Awakening.

Chapter 22
A Sovereign Wizard's Typical Session

Normally I encourage my students to discover their own playful path with Magical Awakening, a path not too restricted by premeditated guidelines. Although I give pointers to what is possible, I always think the best teacher for any student is the energy itself, and that the student will learn most deeply by playing with the energy consistently over a period of time. That being said, even though you are now a Sovereign Wizard it is good to have at least a framework for what a typical Sovereign Wizard session would be. This framework is the same whether you are sending Magical Awakening to yourself, another individual, or a group. Below is a rough outline for offering a typical session.

Start by using any of the relaxing/clearing Enchantments such as angel fire (fire), chakra clearing (fire), bringing the mind into stillness and peace (air), bringing serenity to the emotional body (water), physical relaxation (earth), gemstone properties...but make sure you know the property of the gemstone energy you call forth (earth). This takes one to five minutes depending on how many enchantments are used.

Send Dragon Fire for ten minutes through the entire system to warm the system and prepare it for deeper work. Also intend to burn away and clear out any negative energy (thought forms/anything harmful/etc.).

Call forth a specific issue using the appropriate elemental enchantment: water for emotions, air for mental patterns and conditioning, earth for physical body, fire for anything related to will or purpose. This should take only a minute or two.

Send Arthur's Crown into the issue to awaken it back into Divine Oneness. Allow five to ten minutes for this to happen.

Use Excalibur to release any karmic issues that are ready to be released at this time. Do this by visualizing the person's spine inside of Excalibur. Hold this for three to five minutes. Then, shift intention to release any karmic conditioning that is attached to the issues that have been cleared out, again, for three to five minutes.

Access the Magical Jewels of The Grail to send for five minutes for any relationship issues or healing that requires balancing the relationship between people, organs or organ systems, entities, realms or dimensions simultaneously. Also, simply go into surrender and intend the jewels to work on whatever is needed even if there is no specific issue you are intending to work on.

Send the Grail to the entire system to help the mind/body/spirit know itself as whole and Divine. Do this for approximately seven minutes.

Use the inside of the Grail for integration, approximately five minutes but may vary depending on depth of the healing and ability of the person's energy system to integrate.

For ending options, use any combination of the following: use Mists of Avalon to take the person deeper into Divine Mystery; use earth enchantment on person for self-love of the body; use air enchantment to bring the mind into the absolute present; use water enchantment to call forth internal bath/holy spring or waterfall for purification and refreshing the whole energy system; use fire to awaken person to their own Divine will.

Grounding/Energizing: Use earth enchantment for grounding and a fire enchantment for energizing as the final two aspects of any session.

The Sovereign Wizard's typical session offers plenty of room for improvisation, and also encourages it. Know you should always listen to the energy itself. If the energy is telling you to bypass one of the suggested options, then do so. Let your intuition and the energy guide you. Let it speak to you. In this deep place of listening you will come to possible ways of using the energy in any given specific session that I as the author of this book cannot predict. Just know that those amazing possibilities are there.

Chapter 23
How to Address a Healing Crisis

Magical Awakening always works for the highest good. With that understanding, a healing wizard should always feel free to play and allow his or her own imagination to dance energetically with the imagination of the Divine. The only less than desirable effect that can sometimes happen during a session is that Magical Awakening can in rare instances cause a healing crisis in the person who is receiving a session, especially when Excalibur is used. This happens only when you use Excalibur or another tool for too long, and that normally happens only when not listening to the energy itself. The few times I have energetically caused a healing crisis in someone was when the energy was telling me to stop and I didn't listen. This is one of the reasons I always say to listen to the energy above anything I have written, or anything you might think needs to happen. The energy itself knows beyond all else what to do. When a person is energetically overwhelmed and goes into a healing crisis it means that more unresolved emotion or energetic trauma is being released than the person can easily process. It may present itself as a person feeling old, unpleasant emotions rise to the surface, which on one level is good because they are coming to the surface to be released and healed. Yet, on the other hand, this can feel uncomfortable for that person, and if they are not properly prepared during this time also lead them to panic that somehow the energy healing has gone awry.

If that happens, know that you can wave Merlin's Wand intending that any energies that have been sent that were too much be immediately released. Also, putting a person back into the Grail for integration and using an enchantment of the element of earth to create a grounding cord to make them feel grounded and centered is helpful. Other options that can assist are using the element of air to keep bringing a person back into a place of stillness and inner peace. Again, know that in the end, even if someone is overwhelmed and in a healing crisis, all that means is that there is a profound healing happening, and that the outer symptoms are radically coming up to the surface as part of the healing process. A healing crisis is often considered normal for some energy healing modalities such as Reiki. In Magical Awakening, if you truly listen to the energy such symptoms can be avoided. Again, be reminded that even in the most dire healing crisis, the deep energetic purge that is happening is still for the highest good, just that it may be quite uncomfortable for the person experiencing it. Since we are compassionate wizards, it is best when that sense of discomfort can be avoided or alleviated. Listening to the energy itself is the best prevention. Yet if a healing crises does occur, know you can use the techniques mentioned above to address it.

Chapter 24
Sitting at the Round Table

King Arthur's legendary Round Table holds mythic power in our collective imagination. Whether it ever existed in the historical sense or not, the Round Table implies equality, chivalry, honor, a quest for something higher than ourselves, as well as a collective presence beyond the sum of our individual personalities. My hope in writing this book is not simply to share some wonderful energy healing secrets, but also to inspire a change in society. That change is not just a political or economic change, but a change in imagination. We have so much more that is possible than our social conditioning often allows us to explore. Being a wizard means more than just playing with magic or building up a magically sized ego as some unfortunately do. A wizard's work is to inspire, to be magical, and to live a life that is itself like a work of art. A wizard's work is to laugh, to make others believe in themselves, and to point toward the keys of happiness that live inside each of us. A wizard should be like a child, never take themselves too seriously, and yet always be working magic for the greatest good of the people, including the people who are not in human form but are in animal form, plant form, or those people who exist in other realms such as elves and fairies. A wizard should have a wide imagination and reach their thoughts to the stars knowing that all things in this universe have a consciousness, even your automobile, your laptop, and your water bottle, not to mention the trees, plants, and animals that we share this planet with.

The Round Table implies that we are not only equals with other wizards, other knights, kings, or queens, but that we are also equals with the janitor, the person who washes dishes at our favorite restaurant, those who are farmworkers and truck drivers and nurses. We are equals with animals, plants, and yet that also means we are equals with unicorns and dragons, angels, and the spirit beings who speak to us in our dreams. For the Round Table has no beginning and no end. It is a wonderful metaphor of zero, emptiness, as well as the circle that includes everything.

Sitting at the Round Table is simply a choice. If you want to be a wizard of the Round Table, simply live by the code below:

MAGICAL AWAKENING WIZARD'S CODE

1) Respect and honor the free will of others, as well as yourself. Avoid imposing your will on another.
2) Be honest.

3) Be aware of your power and your position. Do not use Magical Awakening for show, to gain favor of others, nor to impress.

4) Be humble.

5) Always work for the highest good of all.

6) Be noble in your words, compassionate in your thoughts, selfless in your actions.

7) Act your age whenever possible...yet knowing your real age is eternal.

8) Blame no one, not even yourself. For that is to assume you know.

9) Honor the web of life in all of its forms.

10) Know that your life is a riddle, the laughter from a Mobius strip smile that never ends.

Chapter 25
Healing The Wasteland

We live in a spiritual wasteland. This wasteland is in our collective mind, a mindset that encourages a disposable lifestyle and holds little reverence for the very Earth we live upon. We enjoy cartoon heroes, chase phantoms of success, and gawk at photoshopped models as though they were Goddesses to be worshiped. There is something deep and troubling about the way of the modern human and the level of disconnection between our everyday affairs and the larger picture of life on the planet. And often we act as though these two hold no relationship to each other.

Yet you, wizard, have the power to change this. How? You ask how? By being magical. By being so magical that the world that is inspired, as my friend Julia Butterfly Hill often says: stop watching television and go out into the world and tell a vision. Be so magical that your neighbors want to know what it is you do that makes you live the way you do. They will know. They will see that sparkle in your eye that they don't see in anyone else. They will question. They will want to know how they can taste what it is that emanates from your fingertips, from the way you walk, from the calmness you exude. I used to think that if we had enough wizards or Reiki masters or shamans sending energy to heal the world that the world would become healed. And even though that magical energetic equation is entirely true if the numbers were to grow large enough, that isn't how the world will change. The world will change by us offering a more exciting dream, one that is far more real than the dream society has given us. And so I offer you this magical awakening to replace the dream state many have fallen into. Awaken to your own energetic magic, knowing that you have Divine energy hardwired into your energetic system. Know that you can call upon the elements through something as simple as wiggling your fingers. Know that you can release your karmic conditioning created over lifetimes by using the tools you have learned in this book. Know that you can energetically dance with the Divine from moment to moment. Liberate yourself from the slumber, from the idea that you were born only to consume material goods and to meet the expectations of others. Allow yourself to live a magical life. And once you are liberated, others will notice.

That doesn't mean you have to move to an organic farm or live on a commune, though you may if you wish. It means that you can just show up differently, wherever you are. You can walk into work and allow your magic to fill the workplace, even if you never mention being a wizard or never mention this book. You can show up, be wise, inspire others, speak your truth.

At the same time, you can perform magical energy healing to assist your family, your community, as well as the land in the area where you live. You can offer group healings to any collection of individuals, though you should ask for their permission to do so. Invite people over to your apartment or home and offer them a Magical Awakening session to inspire their own magic, to help them be released from that imaginary monster I joke about and refer to as the Dreadlock Octopus, that collection of human thoughts over thousands of years that floats through the ether and attaches to our consciousness like cookies in the internet attaching to your laptop. They aren't necessarily evil thoughts, just that they are taking up all the free space in your mind, and in the mind of the collective. Its time to defrag!

Once a person energetically defrags as an individual they become more alive, more creative, more capable of living a fulfilling magical life that is in harmony with the planet. Some people defrag by meditating, others do it through therapy, and for some others it is done by creating art. And though those methods are entirely valid and useful, I personally find Magical Awakening to be more effective in general. Still, if those other methods work for you, continue using them. There is no need to stop using what already works. But if you want to add some Magical Awakening to defrag, here is a sample protocol for energetically defraging an individual or a group.

The Magical Awakening defrag session begins by the wizard calling upon the enchantment of the element of air to bring to the surface any unuseful thoughts, any coercive images, any outdated belief systems that exist in your mental body. Once you call them to the surface using an enchantment of the element of air, then send Arthur's Crown to wake up those energetic constructs, literally awaken them from the dream they have been promoting. You can also add Excalibur too as a follow up. Intend that your mental body is inside of Excalibur, or use Merlin's wand to invoke Excalibur. Once Excalibur is activated, intend that it purge any unuseful thoughts, outdated belief systems, and coercive images from your mental body. Then follow that by again returning to sending Arthur's Crown into the mental body to smooth out and fill any energetic empty spaces there, because when we release something often it can leave an energetic hole that needs to be filled. If it doesn't get filled, something else will come fill it for you, and it may not be something that is necessarily for your highest good. So, it is always best to fill these empty spaces whenever possible.

Next step for the defrag session is to work on the emotional body. Use an enchantment of the element of water to bring to the surface any emotional conditioning that is not serving any purpose. An example of this is some fear you may have felt when watching a scary R-rated movie as a child. Unless that fear is processed and released it still exists in your emotional body. Most likely, it will not be enough of an issue to ever deal with in therapy or other healing modalities, and so it just stays there, taking up energetic space in your emotional body. Awaken it, and all similar pieces of energetic debris existing in your emotional body by sending Arthur's Crown into all the emotional conditioning that has been brought to the surface. Then, follow up again by sending Excalibur into the emotional body, using Merlin's Wand, or by intending that your emotional body is inside of Excalibur. Once this sword of light is activated, intend that it purge from your emotional body all energetic emotional constructs that serve no real purpose: all emotional hooks from teachers, friends, and family; emotional manipulation by the media; all inherited emotions from your ancestral lineage that serve no higher purpose. As with the mental body, it is important to fill any empty space with Arthur's Crown once you have performed a purge with Excalibur.

Now, use the element of fire to bring to the surface anyone else's will that has been projected into your entire being, including your mental body, emotional body, and physical body. This can be the will of a parent or teacher, a boss or co-worker, the will of an advertising executive who wants you to buy their product, the will of a lover or friend who wants you to act or be a certain way. So often we are influenced by the projections of others' will upon us without even knowing it. How many women starve themselves because the media is projecting an unhealthy and unattainable body image upon them? How many men hold in their emotions because of the collective projections of parents and teachers who didn't want them to express affection or cry? Those are all just projections of other people's will influencing us, and we can energetically adjust the equation so that those energetic invasions, or what I like to call tentacles of the Dreadlock Octopus, aren't holding us hostage. Once you have used the enchantment of the element of fire to bring to the surface all these projections, then use Arthur's Crown to wake them up. Know that in waking them up all you are doing is waking up that energy that is in your own field. It will not necessarily wake up the mind or will of the person (or people) who created the original projection. Still, by waking it up in your own energy field you can be free of it. Once you have sent Arthur's Crown, then follow by invoking Excalibur to purge any projections of other people's will from your entire being. Then follow again with Arthur's Crown to fill in any empty spaces.

This defraging practice is one that if done consistently over time helps to clear our emotions, thoughts, even our physical bodies. It is especially important for women and for men to use them in the region of their pelvis or other sexualized regions of the body to clear away unwanted gender biased judgments, attractions, imposed belief systems, etc. Most often, we hold gender bias based projections in areas of our bodies that easily identify our gender. You can also send Dragon Fire to these regions for additional clearing of others' thoughts, projections, judgments, etc.

As you work on yourself, you will find that this kind of energetic defraging becomes less and less involved, yet it is still important to continue with it as a regular practice. If using the defraging technique on other individuals or on a group, the techniques used are exactly the same. And, fortunately, the size of the group does not seem to require any additional effort on the part of the healing wizard. The real magic after all is coming from Merlin and Lady of the Lake.

Chapter 26
Clearing the Land

A good practice to have as a wizard is to create a deep and ongoing relationship with the land on which you live. You can do that be walking it, getting to know the plants and animals that occupy the land. Even if you live in a city, notice the grass that peaks through the cracks in the sidewalk and the birds that live on the rooftop of the nearest building. Be in touch with the aliveness of nature! Then, make a practice of offering regular Magical Awakening energy treatments to the land itself. You can work on a region of several acres or a couple hundred acres, whatever feels right to you.

Energetically working to heal the land is simple. Begin by sending Dragon Fire out from the cauldron at the belly then down through the ground. Imagine it going down, deep into the Earth. Then, as you are sending Dragon Fire into the Earth, simultaneously create an enchantment of the element of fire, seeing this fire move out through your fingertips down into the ground, moving in synchronicity with the Dragon Fire energy from the cauldron at your navel. Then, intend that this enchantment of the element of fire coming out of your fingertips is connecting with the roots of the nearest trees. Intend then that the trees, which are magical beings according to more shamanic traditions, gather and redistribute all the cleansing fire energy you are sending, both as Dragon Fire and as the element of fire. Allow the trees to do the redistribution, as they know more about the land than we humans usually do. They will know where the lay lines exist, where the underground rivers may flow. Give all this energy to the trees, through their roots, and ask them to perform the cleansing. Intend that the trees include any manmade structures in the cleansing, so that they are also cleansing buildings, fences, and other structures during the treatment. Do this treatment for about five minutes.

If you want to add other options, you can call forth the element of earth as selenite, and intend that the land and all buildings are covered with this energetically cleansing crystal. Or, you can use the element of water and intend that it is washing the land free from any negative vibrations. Allow yourself to be imaginative and to play. Use the element of air as the mantra Om to deepen into the land the level of healing and cleansing. Play, and yet be reverent of the land, intending to clear it. Once you have finished, take a walk in your neighborhood and notice how the vibration feels. How does the air feel? How do your feet feel standing upon the ground? Just notice, and then imagine. The possibilities are endless.

Chapter 27
Unfolding into the Field of Magical Play

Your ability as a wizard in this lineage called Magical Awakening does not stop with you simply acquiring the energetic tools of the first three levels. There are in fact many more tools in this lineage than are made available through this book. If you want to go further acquiring more energetic tools and getting trained in person, take the opportunity to study with one of the Magical Awakening teachers. There are several in the United States, one in Canada, and one in the UK, though I expect that their numbers will surely grow. Those teachers officially trained and endorsed by me can be found on the website www.magicalawakening.org. Still, even if you decide not to pursue further training, you can continuously grow your abilities by unfolding into the field of magical play. For me, this is a metaphor for the way I see life.

First, know that you are not alone in this universe. You are made of magical light and Divine consciousness. The very fact that you exist is an act of magic. Make a daily practice of playing with the Magical Awakening energy that you now have access to. Know that you are an energy transformer. You can do great work, healing yourself and others with the tools you already have. But your abilities and range of how you can use those tools can grow even without you taking on further levels of study.

Many years ago when I was studying Wicca a fellow seeker in that path once reminded me that it isn't how much magic you know that is important. What is important is knowing when and where to send it. She was right, and I often am reminded of this: sometimes the most profound healings and transformational acts of magic happen not because someone had higher levels of training but simply because they used the energy with wisdom and picked the right tool available to them at the right time.

That ability to know when to use a specific type of energy, whether to use the element of air, or Excalibur, or any other Magical Awakening tool, will come to you by deep listening and by play. So, you have to expand that range of play. Take it outside the clinical healing space and make it part of your life. Try intending that you will use Magical Awakening ten times a day for just one day. Then see how those ten uses change your experience of that day, making it more alive. It will entice you then to commit to using it more the next day, and the following day after that, until you are using Magical Awakening as a tool of everyday life.

Know that you no longer have an excuse to be bored. You have the Grand Canyon at your fingertips. You have all the music written by Mozart, Beethoven, Bob Marley, The Beatles, Ella Fitzgerald, all the music that has ever existed in time is available as an energetic signature now through your fingertips. Every herb on the planet is now available as an energetic signature through your fingertips. Every poem every written, every mantra, every magical incantation now exists as an energetic signature that can flow out of your fingertips. Every crystal and gemstone known to humanity, and every mineral too is now energetically available through your fingertips. Each sacred spring, and each pond, lake, sea, and ocean is energetically available to you now. Each line of sacred scripture from all the world's religions can now flow as an energetic signature out of your fingertips. And the list goes on and on.

Not only are you blessed with an unlimited number of energetic options, but if you allow your imagination to take hold and fly with this potential, you can experiment with endless combinations. You can be riding the subway and sending Beethoven's symphonies energetically into the subway car, just to change the energetic ambiance to make it come alive and take it out of the mundane. You can be walking down the street and bring your awareness into deeper communication with the birds, dogs, cats, trees, anything you see by using the element of air. And it is in allowing yourself to spring forth with your magic at these improvisational moments that you will come to understand the true power of this lineage and all that it offers.

Own your magic! Be extraordinary! Don't think, just allow your cosmic imagination to explode. Spend a morning using Excalibur to cut a magical path into your day. Just shake Merlin's Wand a few times, and intend that Excalibur is cutting away the dross of boredom, the unimaginative and conditioned responses that so often consume each moment. And with a flick of your wrist you can liberate those moments. Magical Awakening is much more than just an amazing energy healing modality. It is a way of being in the world. And if I didn't point that out to you I would be failing you miserably. Go forth and fly, and let your imagination soar. Know that each molecule in the universe is aware of every other molecule. Know that the stars, planets, and trees are conscious and alive beings that you can work with and communicate with.

I know what I am saying may frighten some. And I do not expect you to take my word for it. Just suspend your judgment for now, and play. The world is far more amazing than we have been lead to believe. We are not accidents in a realm of dead matter. We are playmates in a grand Divine dream, where everything else is also dreaming and ready to play with us as well.

See the universe as your playground. Be amused. And if anyone ever tries to out you in a box, step out of it. Be a magician and become invisible. And if ever you think life has you handcuffed, find a way to work your magic so that those handcuffs dissolve, or your wrists become soft enough to squeeze free, or that the person who was once your jailer is now your secret liberator even if they don't know it.

We are far too serious as human beings. And it is seriousness that has gotten into a serious mess. By being a laughing, dancing wizard who is sovereign of your own destiny, you will know how best to find your way forward and help heal the world.

Go forth now and play!

Chapter 28
Being in the Presence of Lady of the Lake

You have come through the first three levels of Magical Awakening and may be wondering why I ever bothered to mention Lady of the Lake in those initial chapters. The reason is that she rules most of this system once you get past the first three levels. She sometimes will come through into a healing, not as an energy but as a being, as a full presence. She is a guiding force for much of what happens in this system, and is the co-creative partner of this system along with Merlin. It would be a shame for you to move beyond this book and never really engage her presence or her healing power. So, for this chapter I have an exercise that hopefully allows you to experience some of what she has to offer.

I was told when I first began thinking of how to write this book that it should be only the first three levels. The tools and their complexity do not lend themselves to being taught through a book at the levels that are beyond the first three. Even teaching the first three through the form of a book is extremely challenging for me as the author, mostly because the training normally requires extensive practice and play. The intentional lack of a routine requires the wizard to constantly be in the moment with their own intuition. And though this makes one a better healer, putting this system into a linear book form is extremely challenging. Please know that the training for levels four and beyond are ones that I simply cannot write about, not because I am trying to keep a secret but more because I don't know how to explain the possibilities without it being a question and answer dialogue. Still, there are ways that I can allow you to taste the presence of one of the higher level techniques without actually training you to that level. This isn't meant to be a teaser, but is intended to offer you a glimpse of the Lady of the Lake and her amazing gifts, as well as to get to experience her as one of the co-creators of the Magical Awakening system.

The technique I refer to introduces you to the presence of the Lady of the Lake. In the fourth level of Magical Awakening there is a technique that is taught for calling forth the Lady of the Lake. She has a choice in the matter and may not always come forth. When Lady of the Lake does come forth, it is never clear what she is going to do in the healing. Sometimes I have seen her bless people, often combing their hair energetically or blessing them in other nurturing ways. Other times I have seen Lady of the Lake perform shamanic extractions, pulling out negative energies or entities from a person's energy field.

Other times she has done things that I cannot truly give words to, for fear they wouldn't capture the true sense of what I witnessed.

If you would like to experience a healing from the presence of Lady of the Lake, touch the image below. This book itself is empowered to very high levels of Magical Awakening. And it is through this book that the technique is being implemented, due to some magical wizardry that has happened to the book during the writing of this text. It is the book, not the wingdings image below, that actually is the vehicle for calling in Lady of the Lake. All that happens by you touching the image is that it intersects you with a bit of magic that the book itself is attempting, which in this instance is sending a request to Lady of the Lake to come forth. Please know however that the Lady of the Lake may decide not to come out, and even if she does it usually is only for a few short seconds as the work she does is incredibly fast. She is a being with her own free will, and is not an energy or a pet to be summoned. Even at higher levels of Magical Awakening she has to be asked if she wants to come through, and cannot be summoned through Merlin's Wand as if she were just energy. She is an avatar, a Divine being always to be respected. If she doesn't come out it doesn't mean she never will, so feel free to try again in the future even if it doesn't work the first time. And, if you try to use this as a parlor trick for amusement or entertainment, know she will not come out at all. Before touching the image however, hold an intention that you would like to be healed, or a question which you would like to be enlightened about. Then, respectfully and with deep reverence, touch the image below:

Chapter 29
Healing Phrases and Passages

This book is a healer, a magical being, a wizard in its own right. What follows are healing phrases and passages that you can read, and thus receive energy healings directly from the book as you are reading the phrases and passages. Remember, in shamanic wisdom traditions everything has a consciousness, as does this book. This book is empowered to very high levels of Magical Awakening, and in fact is your actual teacher. Unlike some of my other books, where I have sent the empowerment through time and space to anyone engaging in a particular act that intersects with the empowerment, in this book I have not used that technique. This book itself is empowered as a Magical Awakening teacher. All I have done is intend in writing the book that it empower others at the appropriate times to the appropriate levels.

What follows are some passages where the book itself is sending you healing energy as you read each phrase or passage. Know that you can use these passages for playing at even deeper levels with the energy.

This book is sending Dragon Fire energy now to all who are reading this passage. The Dragon Fire energy is being sent first to your eyes. Now, it is being sent to your spine. Now, it is being sent to your mental body. Now, it is being sent to your gates of consciousness. This book is sending you Dragon Fire directly into your digestive system. This book is sending you Dragon Fire to clear your aura of negative and unwanted energies. This book is sending Dragon Fire to clean your chakras.

This book is now sending you Grail energy into all of your muscles. It is sending Grail energy into your brain and nervous system. It is sending Grail energy to your skeletal system. This book is sending Grail energy into your respiratory system, as well as your circulatory system. This book is sending Grail energy into your emotional body.

This book is sending you Arthur's Crown energy into your karmic body. Think of a specific karmic issue in your life and this book will send Arthur's Crown energy into the karmic root of that issue.

This book is sending Arthur's Crown energy into your mental and emotional bodies. This book is sending Arthur's Crown energy to all energetic veils that are holding you in the dream of being separate from the Divine.

This book is sending you the element of air to bring your mind into a place of stillness and inner peace.

This book is sending you the element of water to bring your emotional body into a place of deep serenity.

This book is sending you the element of fire as an aarti flame to purify your entire being.

This book is sending you the element of earth as the crystal rose quartz to open you to love.

This book is sending you the element of earth as the herb valerian to relax your physical body.

This book is sending you the element of fire as angel fire to clear any remaining negative energy.

This book is sending you the element of water as the holy water of Tempak Sering.

This book is sending you the element of air as the rune charm for healing, Uruz, Sowulo, Jera.

This book is sending you the Mists of Avalon.

This book is putting all of your organs and all your vertebra into Magical Jewels of the Grail.

This book is sending Excalibur into your karmic body.

This book is sending energy from a higher level Magical Awakening tool called Multi-Dimensional Yes through your entire being.

This book is sending energy from a higher level Magical Awakening tool called the Heavenly Ball of Light to you now.

This book is sending energy from you a higher level Magical Awakening tool called the Pool of Light.

This book is sending you energy from a higher level Magical Awakening tool called the Pool of Color.

This book is sending you energy from a higher level Magical Awakening tool called the Pool of Sound.

This book is sending you the energy of Divine Breath, another higher level tool in Magical Awakening.

This book is now putting you into the Grail for integration.

This book is creating a grounding cord from your root chakra to the center of the earth using an enchantment of the element of earth.

This book is sending you Mists of Avalon.

This book is sending you an enchantment of the element of air as the mantra Om.

This book is sending you an enchantment of the element of water as Niagara Falls washing through your chakras.

This book is sending you the element of fire to energize your entire being.

This book is now once again putting you into the Grail for integration.

Stop reading, close this book, and take your time to return from the healing.

Chapter 30
Imagine

Imagine you were born on a planet where most the population, at least the human population, had forgotten they were made of magical light. Wouldn't it make sense that such a population would ignorantly pillage the very magical ball of light on which they lived? They would ignorantly destroy much of it, because they had forgotten that they and the ball were magical. Then, one day, that light was returned to you. And hopefully to many. So that human beings could once again know that they were made out of magical light and had access to this magic. This magic would teach them that life was playful, not serious. This light would teach them that the Divine was whimsical, not an angry God needing to be bowed down to, and that our real purpose in life was to be in playful relationship with all things, the way children can be when their imaginations are unlimited.

You are a wizard now, a sovereign wizard! Go play with the universe, or be an energy healer...there is no real difference between the two. Transform, awaken. Be the magic!

Know as well that this book is more than a book, but is also a magical device imbued with Divine magical consciousness. This book wants to be read, and be seen. It is constantly sending the energy of Excalibur to cut a path of magical liberation for all who read it. It is also always sending higher level Magical Awakening Alchemy of the Grail energies to the path of its own success, to reach as many people on the planet as it can. Hopefully, you will be changed with this book. You will read it, play with it. You can even sleep with it under your pillow and ask it to send healing to you while you dream. Or, just hold it in your hands and ask it to send you an energy healing anytime you wish. To receive an energy healing from the book simply hold it in your hands (or hold ebook device if reading the ebook version) and say the following:

I would like to receive an energy healing from this book for the next (specify number) minutes.

Then let go, relax, and allow the Divine energy healing called Magical Awakening engulf your entire being. Since the book is imbued with Divine magical consciousness, you do not even need to specify what type of Magical Awakening energy is best for it to send. The consciousness in the book will know what you need. Ask, and you shall receive.

Printed in the USA
CPSIA information can be obtained
at www.ICGtesting.com
JSHW011910230424
61721JS00015B/309